Serious Play

An Annotated Guide to Traditional Front Range Classics 5.2-5.9

D1603330

SHARP END PUBLISHING
guidebooks and more
read up
tie in
climb on
PO Box 1613, Boulder, CO 80306
tel: 303.444.2698 fax: 303.413.9757
for more info or samples of our 20+ titles visit
www.sharpendbooks.com

ISBN 1892540-24-X

Cover artwork by Steve Dieckhoff

Title page: Fred Knapp and Sharon Vaughan on The North Ridge, Montezuma's Tower,
Garden of the Gods; photo by Stewart M. Green

READ THIS BEFORE USING THIS BOOK

WARNING:

Climbing is a very dangerous activity. Take all precautions and evaluate your ability
carefully. Use judgment rather than the opinions represented in this book. The
publisher and author assume no responsibility for injury or death resulting from the
use of this book. This book is based on opinions. Do not rely on information, descriptions, or difficulty ratings as these are entirely subjective. If you are unwilling to
assume complete responsibility for your safety, do not use this guide book.

THE AUTHOR AND PUBLISHER EXPRESSLY DISCLAIM ALL REPRESEN-
TATIONS AND WARRANTIES REGARDING THIS GUIDE, THE ACCURACY
OF THE INFORMATION HEREIN, AND THE RESULTS OF YOUR USE
HEREOF, INCLUDING WITHOUT LIMITATION, IMPLIED WARRANTIES
OF MERCHANTABILITY AND FITNESS FOR A PARTICULAR PURPOSE.
THE USER ASSUMES ALL RISK ASSOCIATED WITH THE USE OF THIS
GUIDE.

It is your responsibility to take care of yourself while climbing. Seek a professional
instructor or guide if you are unsure of your ability to handle any circumstances that
may arise. This guide is no substitute for actual lessons.

TABLE OF CONTENTS

SPECIAL INFORMATION

Foreword

by Matt Samet

If you've bought this book then you're probably curious enough about traditional climbing to want to improve. Or maybe you're just bored with sport climbing and want a little more freedom when you climb. In either case, congratulations! Welcome to the world of rock climbing as it was in America until the late 80s . . . and welcome to an endless supply of incredible routes, where savvy, courage, self-confidence and skill will take you further than simple animal strength.

I've been climbing with Steve for two years now, and though I've seen him clip the occasional bolt, his real love is traditional climbing, an arena he excels at. On a recent trip up the two-pitch Blackwalk (5.10 R) in Eldorado Springs Canyon with Steve we had a minor epic, yet it drove home a very salient point—to be a competent, well-rounded rock climber you must develop your traditional climbing skills.

From Blackwalk we had traversed over to a bolt anchor on a ledge atop another route and were preparing to rap down after Steve replaced one of the bolt hangers with a chain link. The hangers were the only anchor available, so while Steve worked on unscrewing one hanger with his wrench, we clipped into the other one and stood there on the ledge.

"I think the bolt's turning," I told Steve. The threads were rotating along with the nut and we ran the risk of shearing the bolt.

"Do you think I should stop?" he asked me.

"Nah, give it another half-turn," I said. He yanked the wrench around another 90 degrees and POP! the bolt snapped, and there we were, 200 feet off the deck, clipped to a single bolt.

"Give me the rack," said Steve, "I'll get us out of here." Steve led off through dirty, loose 5.7, placing but two pieces in 60 feet until he could get above me and set a good anchor. Had we been sport climbers we would have rapped, suicidal with a single-point anchor, or else had to call for a rescue.

Yet it was Steve's capabilities as a trad climber that got us out of there. Through this book's series of well-crafted essays, both technical and psychological in their breadth, Steve conveys how to go about developing these skills. There is a process to it . . . a method, and while the gains are slow in trad climbing, the rewards are huge. There is simply no more rewarding experience in the world of roped climbing than the successful completion of a traditional climb. You leave nothing behind—no bolts, no chipped pockets, no foot-long tick marks. Just a few signs of chalk on the edge of a splitter crack, dabs of harmless white that wash off with the next storm. Indeed, this is roped climbing at its best!

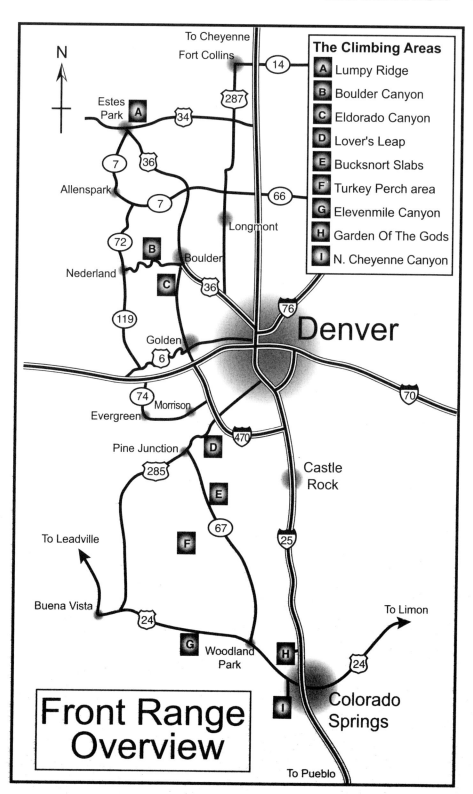

N

The Climbing Areas

A Lumpy Ridge
B Boulder Canyon
C Eldorado Canyon
D Lover's Leap
E Bucksnort Slabs
F Turkey Perch area
G Elevenmile Canyon
H Garden Of The Gods
I N. Cheyenne Canyon

To Cheyenne
Fort Collins

14

287

Estes Park **A**

34

7 36

Allenspark

7

66

Longmont

72 **B**

Boulder

Nederland

C 36

119

76

Denver

Golden

6

74 Morrison

Evergreen

70

470

Pine Junction **D**

285

Castle Rock

E

67

To Leadville

F

25

Buena Vista

24

To Limon

G Woodland Park

H

24

I

To Pueblo

Colorado Springs

Front Range Overview

Introduction

I was lucky. When I enrolled at Prescott College in 1970 I was immediately introduced to rock climbing. The Granite Dells, a labyrinth of nearby granite domes, were mine to explore at ever-increasing angles. Climbing lore was not as available in print as it is today, but a subculture of generous climbers shared their lessons with me—at the time, a raw youth.

I was also lucky enough to witness truly gifted climbers performing their art on the rock, memories of which have inspired me throughout my climbing career. What I've learned through stubborn trial-and-error has been made possible by the stoic patience of my partners, to whom I am forever indebted. My purpose in writing this book is to offer new traditional climbers the same sort of advice, hints, tricks and encouragement that I received from my community. It's still true that good judgment is the product of experience. You can learn something every time you climb.

> *"I meant to tell mankind . . . to attempt a quixotic adventure with no resources beyond their native strength and sagacity. I had done it myself and found not only that the pearl of great price was worth far more than I possessed, but that the very perils and privations of the Quest were themselves my dearest memories. I was certain of this at least: that nothing in the world except this was worth doing."*
>
> *- Aleister Crowley, The Confessions of Aleister Crowley.*

The Art of Leading

What Yogi Berra said of baseball—"It's 50% physical and 90% mental"—applies to climbing as well. During the pioneering days of our sport climbers scaled rocks and peaks using ropes that might break under the stress of a mere 20-foot fall. In lieu of sophisticated climbing equipment, a common practice was for the leader to run the rope over a flake or horn of rock for "protection." In the US, ropes weren't considered trustworthy enough for simple descent until the 1920s. One early (and somewhat painful) rappel technique—the dulfersitz—involved wrapping the rope around your shoulder, waist and groin to produce the necessary friction. Prior to this, downclimbing was often the only way back to the ground.

In the early days of the sport the rope was primarily a safety tool and an aid for the second. Geoffrey Winthrop Young's maxim that "the leader must not fall" was not a matter of style, it was a matter of survival. With the advent of nylon rope during World War II, advancements in pitoncraft, and the concept of the "dynamic belay" put forward by Arnold Wexler in 1947, it became possible to risk a fall under certain circumstances. When I was taught to climb I was taught the hip belay (there were no belay devices then) but was told that if a dynamic belay were necessary the hip belay would default to dynamic.

Risk is intrinsic to climbing and all attempts to eliminate it have fallen short. Like a cut gem, the idea of "calculated risk" is multifaceted. As technology and technique have evolved, safety margins have grown as well. Nonetheless, risk still exists and climbers must learn to assess it move by move, pitch by pitch. Technology simply can't correct a poorly-tied knot, a rope running over a sharp edge or the foibles of an inattentive belayer.

Despite risk, we climb. Our reasons are profoundly personal and may vary from day to day or climb to climb. The traditional climber values the engagement of her imagination demanded by this exacting discipline. Without fixed protection to mark the path she is forced to "read" the rock herself—to find the natural line, anticipating potential cruxes, locating potential rests and fishing in protection. Trad climbs might appear much the same way they did to the first ascensionists. Each pitch is first climbed in the imagination.

We never forget the good climbs. Each one becomes part of our personal history, much as we become part of the route's history, indirectly linked to the others who have climbed it. It's an experience bridging the span of time, profound because it requires the best of us. Simply put, trad climbing demands an awareness and acceptance of risk and the ability to act when the outcome is uncertain.

Learning to Lead

Luck favors the well-prepared. Far removed from the safety and convenience of climbing gyms, traditional climbing requires the ability to weigh a variety of factors. Gyms and sport-climbing may cultivate an appetite for the physical pleasure of moving over rock but the flavor of traditional climbing is far more complex. Rather than feeling daunted by the challenge of these complexities a traditional climber savors the opportunity to thoroughly immerse himself in the experience. The greater your sense of competence the more you can enjoy it. It's a lifelong process.

The first thing to remember is to start easy. Study books on knots and ropework and practice at home. Go bouldering often to become comfortable with a variety of techniques including resting and downclimbing. Choose simple routes to begin with. If your experience thus far has been limited to gyms and sport-climbing then your first dozen "trad" leads should be done on pitches far easier than you ordinarily onsight. The purpose should be to become familiar and comfortable with elements of routefinding and ropework. Longer multi-pitch climbs done further afield will test your navigation and problem-solving abilities and give you the confidence to add the technical challenges of harder routes.

A little clean aid climbing is invaluable in learning how to place good protection and developing your judgment in how good it really is. This is the single best thing you can do for your skill with climbing hardware. You can use a toprope or a fixed line for added safety on your initial experiments before actually leading a pitch.

Climb with a good partner. This doesn't always mean that your partner has to be the most accomplished but that you can trust them to pay attention and communicate well. Enthusiasm is a must. Patience, humor, and the ability to judge when to retreat are all better qualities in a partner than technical ability.

When you are on the sharp end you are doing a balancing act. You are weighing the balance between the quality of your protection and the consequences of a fall. Your ability to execute a series of moves is weighed against the demands of routefinding. On some high-gravity days these decisions are overwhelming and on other days you will flow through the climb seemingly without effort. The study of climbing is a science but the performance of it is an art.

Ratings

The Yosemite Decimal System, the rating system most commonly used in the United States, quantifies the physical difficulty of a rock climb. The ratings used most often on modern rock climbs are 'fifth class,' meaning the leader places gear to protect a fall, not to make upward progress or rest. Pulling or resting on gear is considered aid climbing. The ratings for aid climbs range from A0 to A5 and are contingent upon the holding strength of the gear.

In keeping with accepted laws of mathematics, the fifth class scale originally went from 5.0 to 5.9. The most difficult climbs of the 1950s were rated 5.9. Advances in training and technology helped climbers to push the standards; rather than change the ratings of the existing climbs, a new designation was created—the mathematically implausible 5.10. This trend has continued to the point that 5.14s (and potential 5.15s) now dot the landscape. Further complicating this system is the fact that ratings from 5.10 on up are split into A, B, C or D grades.

At best, this rating system is an indicator of the technical difficulty and/or physicality of a given climb. Ratings are subjective. Many factors influence ratings, and a rating may change over time. A 5.9 slab put up in 1960 could go at a mere 5.7 today because of stickier shoe rubber. Similarly, a 5.9 mantle in done 1960 might now go at 5.11 because mantling has become a lost art.

In addition to a YDS rating, most guidebooks include a rating for the relative seriousness of a pitch based on both rock quality and the quality and availability of protection. In his classic local climbing guide *Rocky Heights*, Jim Erickson borrows the familiar motion picture ratings **PG, R** and **X**. These grades correspond to **safe**, **dangerous**, and **very dangerous** routes. Though **PG** connotes a "safe" route, Erickson continues: "This does not mean that one cannot be hurt on one of these climbs, or that there will be bombproof protection every two feet of the entire climb. It only implies that a deliberate, well-equipped leader should be able to do that particular climb near his limit with a reasonable margin of safety."

A route's difficulty is often a consensus rating, as finger size, hand size and reach vary from person to person. Oftentimes you'll notice that several routes of the same grade seem easier or harder to you. This should teach you to not make assumptions based on ratings. Look for yourself, judge for yourself, and remember that the aesthetics of a route have nothing to do with its grade!

With only a few exceptions, ratings in this book are generally consistent with ratings in other guidebooks. Some pitches or sections of routes may be rated a little higher than in previous descriptions, but I've tried to keep overall route grades the same.

Gear

The basic rack for trad climbing in the Front Range should include:

4 full-length slings (they should fit comfortably over your shoulder)
8 "free" carabiners
1 locking carabiner
RPs #2-#5 or the equivalent
a full set of wired stoppers with extra 1/2"-3/4"
hexes and/or cams 3/4"-4" with extra 3/4"-1" cams
8 quickdraws

a belay device which can also be used for rappelling

a 50-meter (165') rope in good condition; better yet, buy a 60-meter rope, which is more versatile for rappelling

If you consider your brain a vital organ you should wear a helmet! As for shoes you'll have to decide for yourself. Even the best shoes on the market aren't worth much if they're too loose or too tight.

On some pitches you may want extra pieces of a certain size on your rack. For instance, if you fling yourself at the plus-sized Huston Crack you'll need to supplement the "basic rack" listed above with big pieces. It's traditional to borrow gear from your friends in these cases (don't forget to return it!).

You'll have frequent opportunities to bolster your rack by harvesting gear left by others. Bearing that in mind, add a cleaning tool to the list . . .

How to Use this Book

The purpose of this book is to furnish the kind of information, hints, tricks, suggestions and encouragement that I learned from my climbing mentors as a beginning leader.

New trad climbers learning to lead may feel overwhelmed by the variety and abundance of detail before them (as did I when starting) so I've tried to draw attention to some relevant points. This guide does not indicate when a belay must be set up with your own gear. You can assume that if fixed belay anchors are not mentioned you must set a belay from your own anchors.

In addition to the detailed information within the written descriptions, several icons provide route and descent information:

 Face climbing

 Crack climbing

 Inobvious routefinding

 Clean protection

 Descend by rappelling

 Descend by walk-off or scramble

 Possible loose rock

 Gives a reference spot for an action photo location on a drawing

Additionally, each pitch has a symbol to indicate how appropriate it is for a first lead at the grade.

 = good first lead at the grade

 = challenging first lead at the grade

 = not recommended as a first lead at the grade

The best way to choose a route is to study it with your partner. The more time spent visualizing the climb, the greater the return. Factors to consider include the weather, the length of the climb, the difficulty of various sections of the route, the protection and the descent. Climb the route first in your imagination, considering the ideas provided in this guide. If you study the route carefully beforehand, there should be few surprises.

Backword

by Roger "Strappo" Hughes

This essential work authored by Steve Dieckhoff will allow future generations of climbers to master techniques that will take them far beyond the confines of repetitious and often tedious bolt-protected climbing.

Unfortunately, traditional a.k.a. brave climbing is not the type of instant thrill sport to be dabbled in. Indeed, the journey towards competency in rock climbing can amount to nothing more than a long exercise in frustration garnished with an array of epic defeats. But the tenacious pupil will find in his or her EVENTUAL mastery a tool to be wielded in so many far- flung corners of the planet. Please believe me. The rewards will amount to a lifetime of great personal achievement amid these wild places. Is there a finer way to live a life?

But enough about Steve and his book. Let's talk about me.

As a self-taught climber I had to learn from many nearly fatal mistakes that I can still smile about today and would certainly not wish upon my worst enemies. For general interest, here is a brief account of some of those blunders.

As a budding young criminal growing up amid the urban squalor of Liverpool in the early Seventies, my future life was bleak and highly unappealing until that joyful day when I managed to rob a climbing instruction book from the school supply store.

Thus I embarked on a terrifying period of nightmarish self-destruction.

The first of a long catalog of disasterthons took place when I tried to lead my first rock climb, and after wandering completely off the established route, slipped on mossy Welsh permagrease; I plummeted approximately twenty five feet, ripping the three small wired nuts that I had placed for protection. The fourth held me and I went on to make even more lame and totally inept blunders.

Learning to rappel was worse. Unluckily for the male anatomy, roped descents back then were carried out with little regard for the furtherance of humankind, with ropes grinding merrily into genitalia, hipbones, collarbones and other unlikely places.

On that fateful day I slithered painfully earthwards and away from the rock, but the cabled rope began to slice like cheesewire into my exposed neck.

Not feeling ready for complete decapitation at such an early stage in my climbing career I let go with my brake hand (the all-time worst mistake possible) and lunged at the offending garrotte, but I somehow ended up dangling twenty feet off the ground, suspended from the rope cinched tightly around an elbow.

A wave of panic swept over me as my forearms quickly became discolored and numb. In a flash, my partner sprinted around to the anchor and proceeded to mash the rope against the rock with a hammer as I nervously eyed the rocky landing site below me. Suddenly I recalled a vivid image of a diagram in the climbing manual.

"Whoa. Wait a minute. I've got an idea," and in a flash I set up prussik slings on the rope above me and hoisted my weight onto the two hastily-fashioned stirrups. My lifeless arm was saved and the relief immeasurable.

CONCLUSIONS:

1. Don't steal. The bad Karma will come crashing down on you like a ton of feces.

2. Learn all you can as soon as you can so as to cover yourself against the unexpected crises that WILL always assail you when you least expect it.

3. Keep an expert on hand in case you f__k up, but don't use her unless confronted by the icy hand of death.

4. Get to know your limitations, choose your routes thoughtfully and save yourself lots of mind-numbing terror.

Feliz Escalando!

Strappo

Lumpy Ridge

Joyce Bracht on the Hurley Traverse
variation of the Cave Exit, The Book

photo: Crusher Bartlett

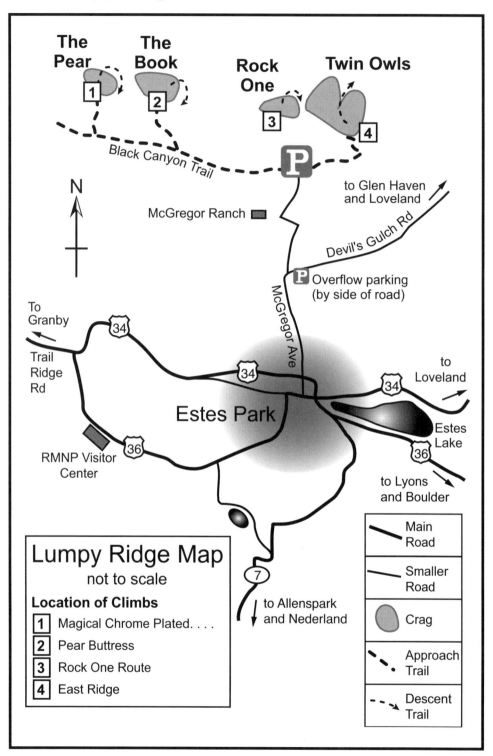

The Pear

The Book

Rock One

Twin Owls

1

2

3

4

Black Canyon Trail

N

McGregor Ranch

P

to Glen Haven and Loveland

Devil's Gulch Rd

P Overflow parking (by side of road)

McGregor Ave

To Granby

34

Trail Ridge Rd

34

Estes Park

to Loveland

34

Estes Lake

36

RMNP Visitor Center

36

to Lyons and Boulder

7

to Allenspark and Nederland

Lumpy Ridge Map

not to scale

Location of Climbs

1	Magical Chrome Plated. . . .
2	Pear Buttress
3	Rock One Route
4	East Ridge

Main Road	
Smaller Road	
Crag	
Approach Trail	
Descent Trail	

Lumpy Ridge

The granite domes and crags of Lumpy Ridge dominate the northern skyline of Estes Park, greeting visitors from the Front Range as they venture to the high peaks of Rocky Mountain National Park. Lumpy has long been a popular practice area for the Park's alpine routes. The southern exposure can mean warm rock in the winter and the higher altitude can be pleasantly cooler in the summer. In the winter the weather can be clear—above the clouds hugging the foothills—but in the summer you need to be alert for thunderstorms. Lumpy, despite its craggy feel, is still a mountain venue and with this comes the weather and altitude risks of the high country. The up side is that the vistas of snow-covered mountains add immeasurably to the quality of the experience.

By and large, climbs at Lumpy Ridge follow flaring cracks that demand a set of skills different from the classic splitters. What appear to be handcracks often accept only fingers; conventional jams are altered to accommodate the widening flares; and secure footing often depends on friction more than pure jamming technique.

Descents at Lumpy Ridge can entail tricky down-climbing and careful navigation through boulders and shrubbery. Even in the best of conditions the process is time-consuming. Under bad conditions (especially if there is snow in the gullies), descending at Lumpy can be down-right treacherous. Sacrificing a sling for a rappel anchor might be the best choice. Descending is part of the climbing experience and should never be taken lightly. Be careful!

The Pear
Magical Chrome Plated Semi-Automatic Enema Syringe

The Pear

This formation is just to the west of the various "Book" formations. Oddly, the Pear Buttress route is not actually found here but on The Book—perhaps this is a practical joke. To reach The Pear hike the main Black Canyon Trail passing the turn-off for The Book. Just after a gate a climbers' trail leads to the crag.

MAGICAL CHROME-PLATED SEMI-AUTOMATIC ENEMA SYRINGE (5.6)

Pitch 1   5.6 ⚜

a. Start atop the megaton block near the bottom of the large left-facing dihedral. You're better off surmounting the block more towards its front than scrambling up the wide cleft behind it (a somewhat dicey proposition without a rope).

b. Several cracks lace the wall above the block. The crack/corner furthest left offers good climbing but is very runout at the start. The crack to its right is the safer choice and goes at 5.5.

c. A fairly easy traverse leads left; try to protect it for your second. A thin, clean flake leads to the belay. Above the flake you'll butt heads with a short runout that feels downright spooky for 5.6+. Compounding your worries, your last piece of gear is in the top of the flake, which seems rather fragile. Draping a sling over the top of the flake might be smarter than placing a cam, which could exert outward force.

d. Alternately, you can traverse past the flake to a series of smaller flakes that lead more directly to a right-facing crack and thence to the belay. Though this option too involves a runout, it's on larger holds.

Pitch 2   5.6 ⚐

e. Climb the right-facing corner above then follow a ledge leftwards to belay beneath the long, left-facing corner with the hand-crack. Note: you can escape here by walking off to the left.

Pitch 3   5.4 ⚐

f. This pitch follows the long corner. Considering its excellent position, bomber gear and clean rock, this is one of the best pitches around for the grade. Ration your gear wisely on this long (full rope-length) pitch. Use small pro whenever possible as this pitch takes bigger gear just about everywhere.

g. Belay in a small niche at the bottom of a crack pointing toward the summit. Should you need to escape, rappel down to the walk-off ledge below you.

Pitch 4   5.5

Follow the excellent crack above past a short, steeper section and a dead tree to a ledge. Belay as far right as is practical without creating rope-drag or communication problems.

Pitch 5   5.6

h. There are several ways to tackle this pitch:

The prominent fist crack bisecting the bulbous roof above is undoubtedly the inspiration for this route's name and goes at 5.9.

Somewhat to the right are a series of right-facing corners. These go at 5.7 or harder; while well-protected and direct, the climbing is fairly problematic through the steepest of the corners.

The third option (which follows what is probably the last pitch of a route called Slippage which comes in from the right), ascends a steep, blocky corner (5.6) and cuts right (crux 5.6) around a large block that isn't as solid as it looks. I can't really recommend this option because of the loose block!

The fourth option "i" is more in keeping with the nature of the route thus far . . . .

i. Follow a thin ledge that diagonals up and right; the traverse goes at about 5.4 or so. Above the ledge climb a 10' section of unprotected 5.5 to reach a thin crack diagonaling up and left to easier ground. The rock is low-angle here; cop a no-hands rest before the runout and get your head together.

Descent: A single-rope rappel (75') from a two-bolt anchor into the gully to the north, then scramble east.

Jim Clark traversing to the first belay.   photo: Roger Clark

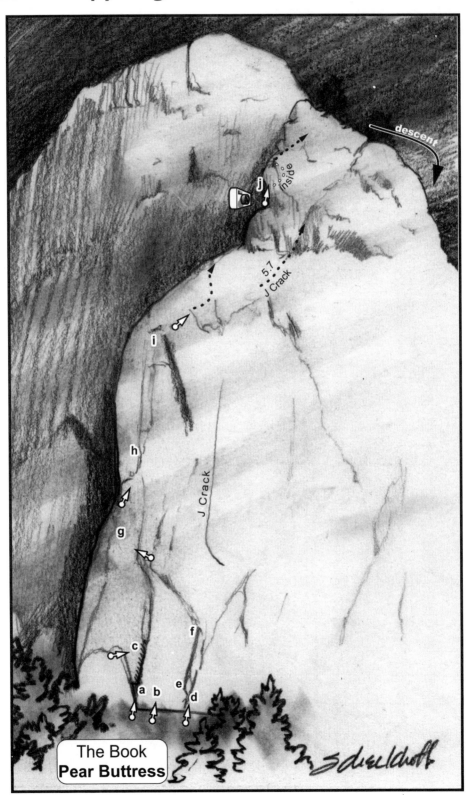

The Book
Pear Buttress

The Book

Literacy flourishes at Lumpy Ridge despite the Internet age. With its many fine multi-pitch climbs, The Book is one of the most popular crags at Lumpy. The landmark route on The Book is J-Crack, identified as a backwards "J" in the middle of a clean face. This is a must-do climb, but you must be prepared for its difficulties and lack of pro. In the meantime tackle the elegant climbing of the adjacent, even-more-popular Pear Buttress.

To reach The Book, follow the main Black Canyon Trail from the parking lot. At a signed climber's access trail, head up the hillside. Take the right fork and follow it to a large boulder. At the boulder head right to the base of Pear Buttress.

PEAR BUTTRESS 5.8+

Pitch 1   5.8+ ❖

There are four options at the start.

a. This option takes the committing natural line up a wide crack, around a small roof and up the corner that is formed by the right side of a 60' flake. This option is 5.9 and involves first placing some small but solid wires in a thin crack that disappears behind the flake. Layback to where the crack narrows and protection may be placed. The laybacking is "thuggish" but solid and blessed with footholds. The edge on the flake is good and gets better the higher you get, but you are still risking a nasty fall during the runout.

b. Climb just right of option **a** on unprotected 5.7 face climbing leading to the place where the crack narrows. The hardest moves are near the bottom, but the section in its entirety requires nerves of steel! It's not really in keeping with the nature of the rest of the leads described in this book so save it for later.

c. This option traverses easily to the top of the flake from the left, eliminating the perils of options **a** and **b.** Hike around the large slabs to your left and go up a gully to reach the left side of the flake. Traverse in to join the route at a set of double cracks and a 5.8+ crux. Continue up, using the best of both cracks to reach a crystalline niche where you belay.

d. The last option, which starts just right and follows the first 5.9 pitch of Loose Ends, is an excellent way to gain the same crystalline niche belay reached by Pear Buttress. Grimp a little ways up the crack to a natural chockstone, which you can sling and/or back up with large cam. Clip in with a long runner to prevent rope-drag.

e. Reach left then step into a long, thin crack in a slender, left-facing corner. Sinker finger locks and bomber gear take you to the spike (**f**) where you'll find a nest of slings. Many parties lower from here, content to have done this 70' pitch as a worthy amusement in itself. You'll get maximum value out of the corner if you climb deliberately, taking the time to scope out and exploit each hand and foot hold!

f. You can set a hanging belay at the slings or continue on via a lengthy, rising traverse to the left. Initially daunting, the 5.8 traverse is actually full of pleasant surprises for your hands, feet and protection. As you glide effortlessly along this traverse, don't forget to protect it for your second. Belay in the crystalline niche.

Pitch 2   5.6 🦂

g. From the crystalline niche traverse left past two finger cracks (Visual Aids, 5.10b, and Loose Ends, 5.9) and find the cleverest path to a ledge just above. This ledge affords a comfortable belay that keeps you in contact with your second. There are also escape possibilities here which involve rappelling into the large corner below. Alternately, continue another 40' and belay at the base of the beautiful finger/hand crack, lengthening this pitch and shortening the next. Unfortunately, this higher belay lacks the suite comfort of the first flat ledge.

Pitch 3   5.8 🦂

h. A short hand crack above the "suite ledge" leads to a sweet finger/hand crack. The climbing here is quintessential Lumpy Ridge, unparalleled for pure fun—except maybe by the enticing corner out right.

i. Several options at the top of the crack lead to the lower-angled climbing below "The Cave." Straight up is 5.8+ R but the best one traverses right beneath the small roof (5.7) and works over to a good belay.

Pitch 4   5.5 ♣

There are various ways to reach the rising ledge/gully above. I recommend the easiest way, which climbs right to another crack that is followed up and left. Watch for loose rock on the ledge/gully. Notice the possibility of traversing further to the right to join the last pitch of J-Crack (5.7).

Pitch 5   5.8 ♣

j. Though perplexing, the notorious Cave Exit is not nearly as extreme as it looks. Stem from a block to a flake to place an overhead cam and/or make a long reach to a fixed pin. Step over to the top of the flake while ducking under the roof above (think Houdini). If you've made it this far, the last 15' of the route will seem fairly pedestrian. Below this pitch is another option; the Hurley Traverse (see photo page 13). This hand traverse is 5.7, but the protection is problematic.

Descent: The well-traveled descent route follows a ledge eastwards before meandering downwards into the obvious gully. In places a careless move could result in injury. Look for the easiest line—not always the most direct—and spot your partner if needed on the slippery down-climbing sections.

Books

Books on climbing generally fall into one of three categories: instructional manuals, guidebooks and story books.

Instructional books are useful for learning knots and a variety of other techniques, some of which you'll use as a matter of routine, some of which you may never use at all. A good instructional book (such as *Mountaineering: Freedom of the Hills*) is worth keeping around as a reference for techniques like self-belaying and self-rescue. Though you may not use them often, these procedures (like all ropework) need to be mastered and held at ready in case of emergency.

The next type of book is the guidebook. Some guidebooks sample the best routes in a given geographic area. Others are more enumerated, detailing each and every route at a single crag. In either case, you can never have too many guidebooks . . . .

The third type of book tells stories or relates climbing history. If we were motivated to climb simply for exercise then there would be no great stories to tell. Reading the stories of others (like my favorite, *The Bat and the Wicked* by Robin Smith) inspires us to tell our own. The best stories are never about easy success. It's often the most miserable, terrifying or absurd events that make for a good story. So, if you find yourself embroiled in some ridiculous epic, just keep telling yourself that "this will make a good story someday!"

Of course the book you are currently reading may qualify as a fourth type of book—a hybrid guidebook and instructional manual designed to teach through experiential learning.

Were it still in print, an integral part of every Front Range climber's library would be *Climb, Rock Climbing in Colorado* by Bob Godfrey and Dudley Chelton. The text gives excellent historical perspective and, along with the many beautiful photographs, provides inspiring insights into a host of seminal routes in Colorado. Look for the updated *Climb II* by Jeff Achey, to be published soon by the Seattle Mountaineers.

Twin Owls
East Ridge

Rock One
Rock One Route

Schulthoff

Rock One

This is the small, separate formation just west of Twin Owls. To reach the crag head east on the Gem Lake Trail and after a short distance turn left onto the Lower Twin Owls climber's access trail. Continue to angle around and then up a prominent gully. Look for a ledge leading to the start of the route—a good place to leave packs. Remember to leave your packs in a spot that can be easily spotted when you descend this gully. Be careful traversing around the corner to the start of the route; rope up if necessary or approach it from a little lower.

THE ROCK ONE ROUTE 5.4

This is a pleasant promenade up a gentle crag. Combine this route with the East Ridge of Twin Owls for a long fun day (see descent notes).

Pitch 1 5.2

a. Traverse out left past a small tree and follow a thin crack.

b. Belay near the top of the large corner on your right.

Pitch 2 5.4

c. The path of least resistance seems to be the crack beside a large dead tree. If the tree is gone it is identified as the lowest-angled crack on the left. A few steep moves (5.4) lead to the ridge.

d. An array of cracks lead upwards; I recommend the thinnest one (5.4). These flaring cracks are best climbed by not pulling yourself too far into them. Use whatever face holds you feel comfortable with and step inside when you need that extra feeling of security.

e. Belay when you get to the ledge.

Pitch 3 5.4

f. A short steep section (5.4) takes you to a pleasant left-facing corner.

g. A belay is possible here if you wish.

Pitch 4 5.3

A short slab leads to the top.

Descent: The summit is close to the Twin Owls formation. Scramble down to the north into the gully between these formations. From here you can scramble down the gully back to your gear. Another descent option is to scramble from the top of the gully up and right onto the obvious ledge at the base of Twin Owls, the "Roosting Ramp." This scenic path (3.2+!) leads past the impressive south face of Twin Owls and heads towards the main trail. It works best if you leave nothing at the base of Rock One so you do not need to backtrack. The Roosting Ramp also allows the easiest passage from Rock One Route to The East Ridge of Twin Owls, if you want to combine these in one day.

Twin Owls

This crag is split into two steep sections and perches on the "Roosting Ramp." As you gaze at the intimidating crack lines of the west-facing wall they stare back at you unblinkingly. "Who?" The notorious Crack of Fear is worth a long look. Derek Hersey, soundly sandbagged by its "mere" 5.10 rating in the guidebook, on-sight soloed this route, scraping his knee so badly he couldn't walk for days. Another crack to covet is Anaconda, an old aid route which was free climbed a few years ago by Alan Lester. The list goes on. . . . (who)

The approach is short, but take care not to contribute needlessly to erosion problems. Trail information is usually posted at the start of the Gem Lake trailhead at the east end of the parking lot. To get to the East Ridge route find the trail which branches off just after a big boulder and just before another boulder. This trail angles back and forth before laying you at the feet of the Crack of Fear. Follow the base of the cliff around to the right to find the East Ridge.

EAST RIDGE 5.8

The first pleasant pitch ascends what I would have called a buttress rather than a ridge. Start just around the corner from the south face.

Pitch 1   5.8 ✿

a. From a small ledge/flake reach up to clip a fixed pin then work out the crux of the climb! After a couple of moves you will be able to get a cam in a 3" wide flared placement. Smooth, controlled climbing for another couple of moves ends the difficulties here.

b. At a horizontal (sort of) crack either continue straight up (5.7) past a pin—back it up—or take the crack which is 12' to the right.

c. Easier climbing (5.5) leads to ledges. From the ledges it is possible to rappel (with one rope) into the gully to the east.

Pitch 2   5.6 ✿

d. It may be expedient to move the belay further up and left on the ledges.

Traverse one of a couple of paths to the left, around the roof-like feature above. If you traverse far enough the climbing will remain solid and moderate. Then weave back right and belay.

Pitch 3   5.5 ⚘

e. The easiest route to the top is on the right side of the roof/bulge band above.

Descent: Head down a large cleft heading northeast between the owls—the "Bowels of the Owls." Although most guidebooks list this as 5.0 it is a diet that is best taken with a grain of salt. Slide down this tract or, if this is too much to stomach, consider your rappel options. Be aware of the possibility of snow and ice here seasonally. If that is the case—and you can check this out before starting the climb—then you'd best rappel after the first pitch.

Boulder Canyon

Climbers in The Owl (5.7), The Dome   photo: Stewart M. Green

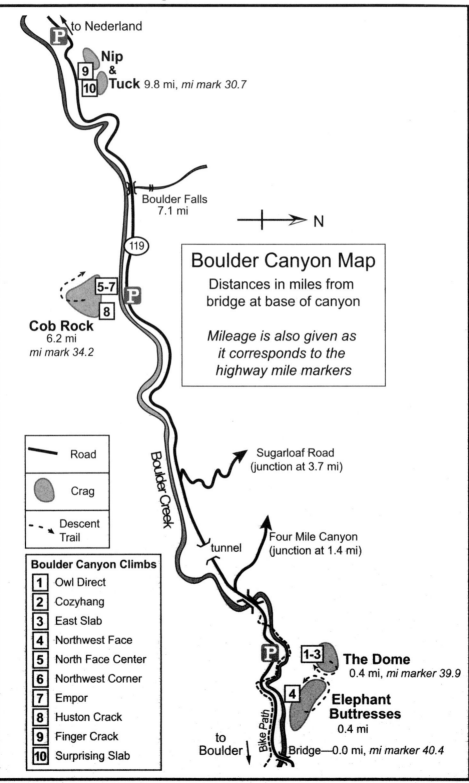

to Nederland

Nip &
Tuck 9.8 mi, *mi mark 30.7*

9
10

Boulder Falls
7.1 mi

→ N

119

5-7
8

Cob Rock
6.2 mi
mi mark 34.2

Boulder Canyon Map
Distances in miles from
bridge at base of canyon

*Mileage is also given as
it corresponds to the
highway mile markers*

Boulder Creek

Road

Crag

Descent
Trail

Sugarloaf Road
(junction at 3.7 mi)

tunnel

Four Mile Canyon
(junction at 1.4 mi)

Boulder Canyon Climbs

1 Owl Direct
2 Cozyhang
3 East Slab
4 Northwest Face
5 North Face Center
6 Northwest Corner
7 Empor
8 Huston Crack
9 Finger Crack
10 Surprising Slab

1-3
4

The Dome
0.4 mi, *mi marker 39.9*

**Elephant
Buttresses**
0.4 mi

to
Boulder

Bike Path

Bridge—0.0 mi, *mi marker 40.4*

Boulder Canyon

This granite canyon winds its way eastward following the path of North Boulder Creek as it leaves Barker Reservoir near Nederland. The canyon is home to numerous crags, from recently developed sport areas to more secluded traditional venues. The classic traditional lines were established decades ago and have long provided Boulderites with the opportunity to practice venerable granite techniques in their backyard. A trio of crags have still maintained their natural ambience, and two lie within a comfortable walk or bike ride from downtown. Cob Rock, The Dome, and the Elephant Buttresses survive like lynx in an urban development.

The canyon's accessibility offers the opportunity to make repeated visits to a particularly problematic route and, by dint of study and willpower, to finally succeed.

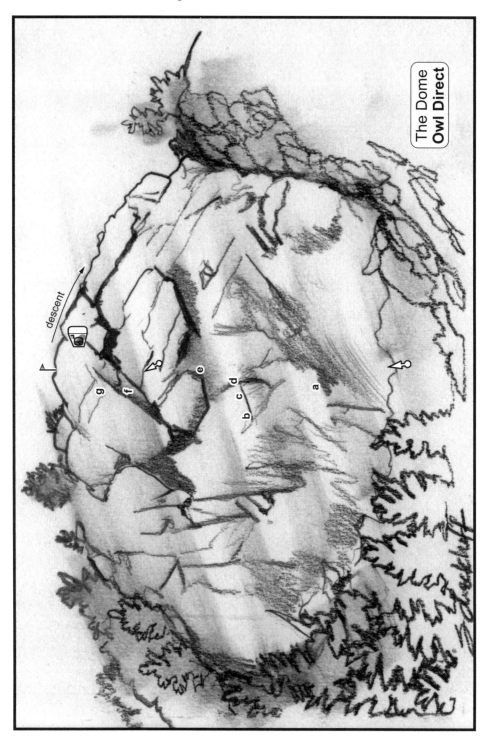

The Dome
Owl Direct

The Dome

THE OWL DIRECT 5.7

This is my favorite route on The Dome.

Pitch 1   5.7 ❖

a. Trend up and left on a diagonaling slab (5.4).

b. Though it seems implausible from the deck, the easiest and most aesthetic route follows a right-leaning crack into the bottom of the prominent, left-facing corner (5.3). The end of the traverse takes great gear.

c. From a stance at the base of the corner head right around the outside of the dihedral. Protect these exciting moves with small wired stoppers and small cams, attaching long slings to prevent rope drag.

d. Swing right onto knobs (5.6) then step right again into a good crack.

e. Climb the crack past an awkward flared section (5.7) to a good belay above.

Pitch 2   5.7+ ❖

f. There are several ways through the overhangs above. The most popular option tackles the crack at the apex of the A-frame roof (5.7, though strenuous for the grade). A more straightforward finish, also 5.7, follows the diagonaling hand crack 25' down and left of the A-frame.

g. Bring enough large gear to protect the hand cracks on the face above (5.3).

Descent: An easy walk-off leads east and then south back to the base.

Kath Pyke on Cozyhang
photo: Andy Donson

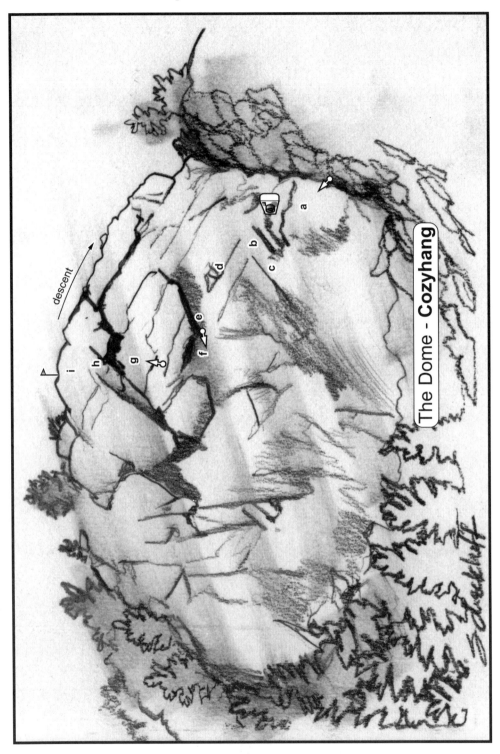

The Dome - Cozyhang

COZYHANG 5.7

This is comfortably challenging, providing cruxes at two different styles of roofs.

Pitch 1 5.7+

a. Follow pleasant cracks just left of the first of three small overlaps.

b. Easily surmount the first two overlaps, saving some gas for the crux third overlap. From a small but secure stance below the third overlap head for the obvious slanting crack in the middle. You can place gear here and study the situation above.

Visualize each hand move of the crux sequence well and don't plug up your jams with gear. You can always downclimb a couple of moves to the rest; the name Cozyhang does not actually refer to resting on gear.

c. If you lack the momentum for the strenuous crack move, dance your way up the thin slab out the left side—a committing, disconcerting option when on lead!

d. Set up a belay immediately above the crux to facilitate communication with your second.

If you've already gotten enough bang for your buck from Cozyhang or you simply need an easy escape, climb a simpler (5.3) but enjoyable pitch past some fixed pins on the right (this avoids the huge roof above).

e. To follow the regular line, diagonal up and left to a snug belay stance (the Cozyhang) below the huge roof.

Pitch 2 5.7

f. The next pitch traverses left and slightly downwards before climbing up to a ledge belay. This 5.7- bit is actually quite challenging. Remember that you should protect a traverse for your second as well as yourself, placing pro both before and after the hard moves.

g. You merge with the Owl route at this point (see notes in the Owl section). The last pitch climbs through the A-frame roof above you. Your belay should be low enough to allow for good communication with your second on pitch 2, yet also permit easy access to the top pitch.

Pitch 3 5.7

h. Though steep and physical, the A-frame roof sports a rest in the middle and is well-protected. It therefore merits a .

Be aware of rope stretch! More rope paid out between you and your belayer equals more rope stretch in a fall. With too much slack you could potentially bottom-out below the roof were you to lob.

i. Mercifully, the angle eases over the roof and it's an easy stroll to the summit.

Descent: An easy walk-off leads east then south back to the base.

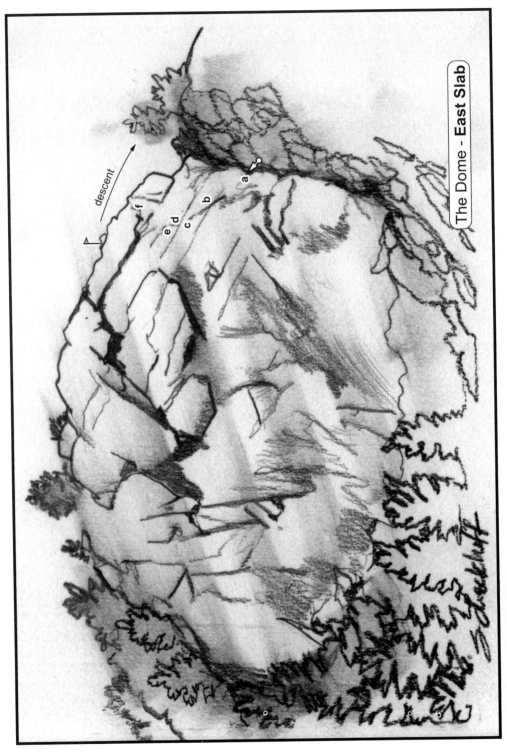

The Dome - East Slab

EAST SLAB (AKA DISAPPEARING CRACK) 5.5 ✤

Don't be fooled by the generic name—this pitch is classic!

a. Start just right of a cleanly-cleaved, prominent 20' dihedral. The easiest route weaves up and left through a blocky section to a stance below the bulging roof at the top of the dihedral (You can climb the dihedral, but it's a little harder.). Your best bet for gear at this point is to place cams in the flaring cracks in front of you and nuts overhead. Continue up and left.

b. Follow the main crack, which is bisected in the middle by a long diagonaling dike.

c. Sink a good piece in the top of the 2.5"-3" crack before casting off on the little runout above (5.5).

d. Though you can stand comfortably at the second diagonal, you'll find that the cracks are too shallow and flaring to take solid gear (the proverbial good stance with bad gear—an all-too-common dilemma in trad climbing!). Stay relaxed—remember, you're standing on huge footholds and the slabby climbing above will feel easier if you remain calm. Your best piece will probably be a 1.5" stopper above you.

e. Shuffle a few feet left along the diagonal and climb straight up on big holds (5.3). Trust your feet.

f. Various well-protected weaknesses breach the summit overhang.

Scrutinize the East Slab and you'll notice that several variations are possible. Explore them if you're feeling adventurous. Study a variant from the ground, comparing its salient features (cracks, slabs, roofs, holds, etc.) to your memory of the standard route. By doing so you can make an educated guess about what the climbing might be like. Toprope the line first to see how close your prediction was before you tackle it on the sharp end. Being able to accurately judge a route from the ground takes practice; you'll get better at it the more you climb.

Descent: an easy walk-off leads east then south back to the base.

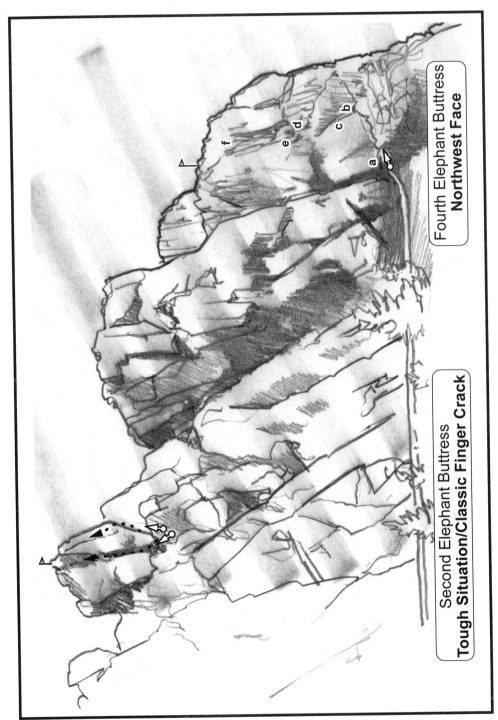

Fourth Elephant Buttress
Northwest Face

Second Elephant Buttress
Tough Situation/Classic Finger Crack

Fourth Elephant Buttress

THE NORTHWEST FACE 5.8

The attention-getting approach along the water pipe and the hyper-convenient location of this popular route contribute as much to its charm as does its excellent climbing.

a. The first crux is the start of the rightward traverse from the water pipe. At least 5.6, these moves may feel harder for shorter folks. Set up a good belay here (think about a sideways/downward pull) or your second risks being violently yarded off the slippery metal of the water pipe should you fall. As always, sink a piece after the hard moves to protect your second.

b. Traverse right about 20' along the obvious break to a thin crack that trends up and left. Belay here if you anticipate rope drag hassles or want to remain in close contact with your second.

c. The thin crack provides a good lesson in difficult protection (you may be able to fiddle a Tricam into a 1 1/2" wide slot). Thankfully, the edges are positive and the climbing only about 5.5. Be aware of rope drag.

d. Weave upwards on slightly steeper rock to arrive at the two "stacked blocks."

e. Even though these blocks have been yanked on for decades — you'll want to use your own judgement. A harder but interesting sequence skirts the blocks on the left. If you climb over the blocks, make a big reach up and left to join the same line.

f. There are a multitude of cracks you can follow to the top from this point. Though it's both safe and instructive to pick your own route, the easiest way trends up and right from crack to crack. Bring a good selection of larger cams for these hand-sized and bigger cracks.

Descent: There are several descents from the top of the Third and Fourth Elephant Buttresses:

1) If the pipeline is dry or you don't mind swimming upstream in the dark then scramble down to the east and follow the tunnel back west. This is quick and fun—two good reasons to do it—but watch your head.

2) Downclimb between the Second and Third Buttresses using some cunning route-finding. Tricky and exposed, this descent is not recommended for beginners.

3) Rappel from a tree between the Second and Third Buttresses.

4) Hike around to the north of the First Elephant Buttress then pick your way down the easy descent gully by The Dome.

Once atop the Elephant Buttresses, many parties opt to toprope and/or lead either Tough Situation 5.9 ♣ or The Classic Finger Crack 5.9 ⚘. Combining these pitches with the Northwest Face of the Fourth Buttress makes for a great outing!

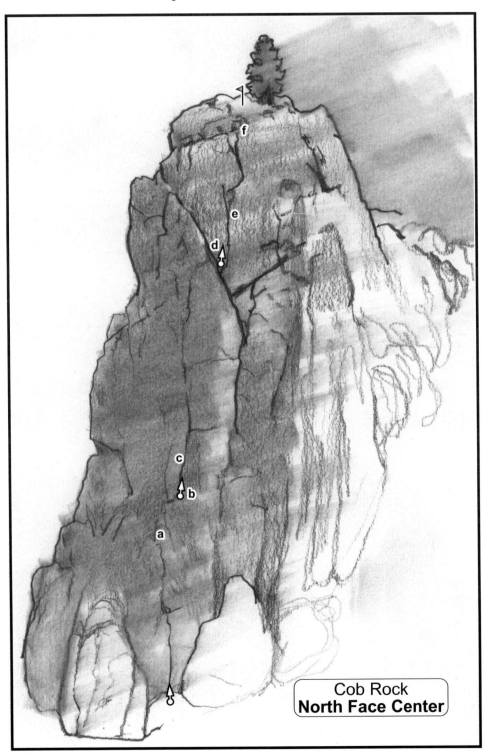

Cob Rock
North Face Center

Cob Rock

Though admittedly smaller, Cob Rock draws the eye of the climber in much the same way as Sentinel Rock in Yosemite. This pleasant chunk of granite offers a variety of moderate routes on good stone, a cool northern exposure, an easy walk-off and an adventurous Tyrolean traverse approach when Boulder Creek is high.

There's usually a fixed rope crossing the river for the Tyrolean traverse. Attach a sling to your harness, clip the rope, and slide across. As an extra precaution, use a locking carabiner to clip the rope. The crossing from the crag to the road is uphill enough that you may have to pull a bit. Use a prussic knot to assist you if you're not strong enough to pull yourself up (have it on-hand and ready-to-go before you find yourself dangling above the water). If your pack is heavy try this trick: clip it in separately and push or pull it across (certainly better than having it drag you ass-backward into the water).

NORTH FACE CENTER 5.7

This is a real classic, with a humble name from simpler times.

Pitch 1 5.6

a. Follow a discontinuous crack rising from the low right-hand corner of the north face. Ample protection and a good supply of face holds supplement the crack. The crux is probably the little step to the right.

b. Belay at a comfortable ledge. You can easily reach this ledge by traversing in from Empor.

Pitch 2 5.7

c. Continue up the obvious crack. The wide section at the bottom is the crux and you will use all the holds available.

d. Belay either at the start of the prominent dihedral or a little further on, depending on which crack you take on the final pitch.

Pitch 3 5.7+

e. The zigzag crack leading to the summit takes protection and hand jams with comforting regularity.

f. Because it's always better to be in sight of your partner, you should belay as soon as you reach horizontal ground rather than up at the large tree. Alternately, pull up about 25' of rope and tie off the tree, leaving enough slack to get you back to the edge. Tie in snugly to the rope, leaving no slack in the belay.

Descend via an easy scramble down from the summit onto the south shoulder, then west and south to a trail along the west side of Cob Rock

Cob Rock - **Empor**

EMPOR 5.7+

Finally, a route with a real name (even though I don't know what it means)!

Pitch 1 5.7+ ❖

a. Begin beneath a massive boulder, stemming and chimneying between it and a right-facing corner to reach its top. Though convoluted, this method is more secure than bouldering up the outside of the boulder.

b. From the top of the boulder tackle the crux, a facey sequence on immaculate stone. Just when you begin to despair a thank-God foothold appears out right.

c. An alternative start follows the right-facing corner from the bottom and goes at 5.8 ❖.

d. Climb to the base of the arching, right-facing dihedral.

Pitch 2 5.4 ⅄

e. Continue up the prominent dihedral to a belay beneath the zigzagging hand crack on the right.

Pitch 3 5.7+ ⅄

f. This crack is described as pitch 3 of the North Face Center route (page 39).

Descent: via an easy scramble down from the summit onto the south shoulder, then west and south to a trail along the west side of Cob Rock.

d

c

b

a

follow first pitch
of **Empor**

Cob Rock
**Northwest
Corner**

Northwest Corner   5.7+

This is yet another excellent route with only a "directional" name. The poetry is in the moves, and they speak for themselves.

Pitch 2   5.7+ ♣

a. From atop the first pitch of Empor (or the direct variation up the corner) follow the path of least resistance up the flakes out to the right; the crack is somewhat harder.

b. A 12' stretch of unprotected but straightforward 5.5+ face moves leads to a horizontal crack. Stay poised! Alternately, you can protect a crack further left that reaches the same horizontal. The horizontal crack takes good gear.

c. Continue up the corner to a short traverse right, ending up at a pair of fixed pins that can be backed up and used as an anchor.

d. The last bulge is a satisfying 5.7.

Descend via an easy scramble down from the summit onto the south shoulder, then west and south to a trail along the west side of Cob Rock.

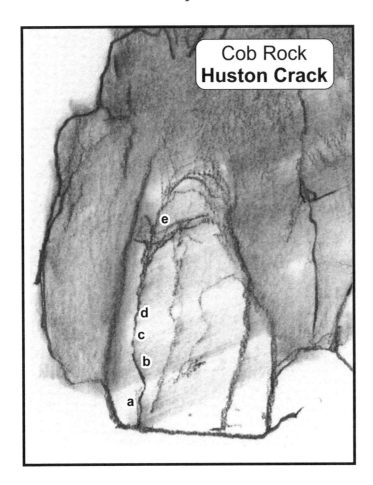

Huston Crack 5.8+

Though christened after first ascensionist Cary Huston, the name of this crack still smacks of the Lone Star state—and sure enough, the crack is Texas-sized! In the past, climbers were more proficient at wide cracks for several reasons. In the mountaineering days of rock climbing, wider cracks were more easily spotted from afar, making them obvious climbing targets. The big stiff boots of the era were better suited for standing comfortably and solidly in these cracks, whereas today's low-profile rock slippers simply "slip" out! Huston Crack is an excellent route for the grade because it forces you to hone your wide crack technique—an invaluable part of your climbing repertoire. A good struggle has its own intrinsic value, and some climbs are so pleasurable that you will want to repeat them again and again.

a. Good hand jams of various sizes lead to an angling 5" crack. The crack takes great large gear, so arm yourself with as many big pieces as you can (you can always borrow from friends).

b. A general rule-of-thumb for crack climbing is to keep your hands low when you step up. Climb with your feet (trust those foot jams) and use your arms and hands for balance as much as possible. Lean left off the angling, wide section; high-step into it, using your calf as a lever against the lower edge of the crack. Once in the crack, experiment with various hand arrangements until you find one that's relatively snug. Maximize your footwork by employing any sort of twisted heel-and-toe jam you can get. Wearing socks (or taping your ankles) will help prevent abrasion if you're wearing dainty, low-topped shoes.

c. You're best off placing your protection far enough back in the crack that you can climb past it without knocking it out yet not so far back that it could get stuck.

d. As you gain proficiency and confidence in your foot-jamming you'll realize that, at this angle (off-vertical), every position is a rest!

e. The end comes much too soon—only 60' up.

Descent: Exit to the left (5.2), and head for the gully.

If you lack the requisite big pro for this pitch you can get above it to set up a toprope by traversing in from the left (5.2).

Just to the right of Huston Crack is the Aid Crack, a frequently-toproped hence highly-polished 5.10d free climb. As an exercise in clean aid, this crack makes for excellent practice with placing and trusting your gear.

Also note that large cams have a propensity to turn sideways in a crack—a problem that small cams do not experience. Long runners are the best way to prevent this.

descent

Nip and Tuck
Finger Crack

Nip and Tuck

A diminutive crag divided in two, this roadside area is easily accessible; it also offers south-facing warmth in the winter and cooler temperatures in the summer due to its altitude. Two routes in particular make great leads. Though short, these pitches have all the makings of classic climbs.

FINGER CRACK 5.9

It's a shame that a route this good should sport such a generic name. I suggest renaming it "Protagonism" in reference to Antagonism, the sport climb to its left.

a. This route is steep, so you'll need to use optimal body positioning to avoid getting pumped. There are four ways to use "finger locks:" left hand thumb-up, left hand thumb-down, right hand thumb-up or right hand thumb-down. Though thumb-up jams generally allow you to crank farther, thumb-down jams are usually more secure. This pitch takes excellent gear, more than enough incentive to commit to the initial steep jams and gain the steep, positive climbing a little higher.

b. This is an excellent pitch on which to practice both "targeting" the next rest and placing gear. The unrelentingly vertical nature of this climb requires that you climb calmly and efficiently. The sinker locks in the crack become increasingly useless the longer you hang out fumbling with gear. Be ready with that next piece! A selection of small-to-medium stoppers should see you through.

c. Though the opening sequence is technically the crux, you may be more challenged by the top of the crack due to its sustained nature. Plug in some half-inch cams here.

Descent: Scramble down the obvious gully.

Nip and Tuck
Surprising Slab

SURPRISING SLAB 5.8

Tricky to protect, this route also boasts a problematic crux. Thankfully, both dilemmas can be solved with grace, as flexibility triumphs over strength.

a. Easier moves low on the route allow you to warm up and get a feel for the stone. The slab's polished surface, sharp edges, large crystals and series of aesthetic horizontals all merge to create a fascinating composition. If you like the feel of this climb then you'll enjoy the Supremacy Slab in Eldorado Canyon.

b. Place your protection in the horizontal cracks. The horizontals are shallow—you'll need a good supply of both patience and ultra-small cams to get your gear in. At the crux section (a body length above the crystalline band) you can comfortably stand around and shuffle back-and-forth as you hunt for pro. Look for a horizontal crack out left after the crux.

c. The small roof, the last of the climbing challenges, is quite pleasant, and the beautiful face climbing below is over much too soon.

You could spend hours toproping different variations on this face, eliminating holds until there are none left. The grace, technique and confidence you learn while mastering this type of climbing will serve you well in your climbing career.

Descend via the obvious scramble down the gully.

Eldorado Canyon

Beth Litchenstein on Wind Ridge   photo: Fred Knapp

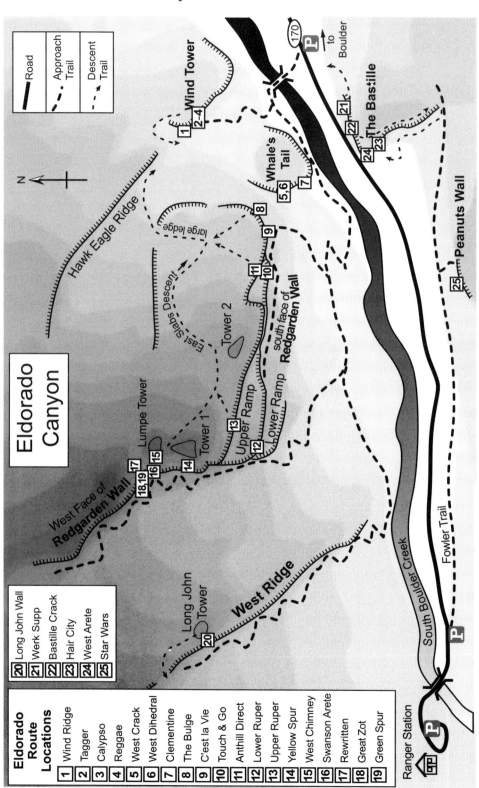

Eldorado Canyon

Road
Approach Trail
Descent Trail

N

Eldorado Route Locations

1 Wind Ridge
2 Tagger
3 Calypso
4 Reggae
5 West Crack
6 West Dihedral
7 Clementine
8 The Bulge
9 C'est la Vie
10 Touch & Go
11 Anthill Direct
12 Lower Ruper
13 Upper Ruper
14 Yellow Spur
15 West Chimney
16 Swanson Arete
17 Rewritten
18 Great Zot
19 Green Spur

20 Long John Wall
21 Werk Supp
22 Bastille Crack
23 Hair City
24 West Arete
25 Star Wars

Wind Tower

Whale's Tail

The Bastille

Peanuts Wall

large ledge

Hawk Eagle Ridge

East Slabs Descent

Tower 2

south face of Redgarden Wall

Lower Ramp

Upper Ramp

Tower 1

Lumpe Tower

West Face of Redgarden Wall

Long John Tower

West Ridge

South Boulder Creek

Fowler Trail

Ranger Station

to Boulder

170

Eldorado Canyon

The name Eldorado comes from the Spanish "City of Gold," an appropriate name given that during the "Golden Age" of rockclimbing in America one of the centers was this canyon of red sandstone. A climber's eye is naturally drawn to the lines of routes like The Naked Edge, Jules Verne, The Yellow Spur, The Wind Ridge and Ruper. These routes achieve a position of particular purity, not only because they represent the remarkable efforts of a generation but because, once you have climbed one and reflect on that experience, you realize they represent some of your best memories as well.

The rock is a very compact sandstone pressured into layers then tilted and sculpted into towers. Unlike the sandstone of the Southwest, Eldorado's Fountain Formation is cemented with aduliria feldspar, offering a hardened stone more similar to quartzite than traditional sandstone. The routes develop a certain cunning in the ability to link features, winkle subtle finesses, and glean protection. Early climbers George Hurley and Pat Ament likened routefinding in the canyon to playing chess—an apt analogy in that you learn to think several moves ahead. This book, in fact, was patterned after books about famous, elegant and instructive chess games.

For first time Eldo climbers, just finding the routes can prove challenging. Because this book has a specific focus and doesn't include neighboring routes, it may be necessary to consult Richard Rossiter's comprehensive guide to locate the start of some routes, especially on the west face of the Redgarden Wall. Don't hesitate to ask other climbers for directions.

Wind Tower
Wind Ridge

The Wind Tower

THE WIND RIDGE **5.6** OR **5.7+**

This multi-pitch classic, offering both fun face and crack climbing, leads to a nice, airy summit. The route follows the protruding horizon line on the north end of the Wind Tower formation.

Pitch 1 5.7 ✤

a. There are three ways to tackle the opening moves. The easiest method is to climb 15' up the dihedral on the left then traverse right above the prominent flake to the arete (5.6). Visualize rope-drag problems before they occur and use long slings where needed.

b. Another alternative is to power up and over the flake (5.7+).

c. The third option is an elegant traverse beneath the flake (5.7).

d. This suspect block should be treated with caution.

e. There are only a few good anchor placements. Your best options are a 1.25" crack here and a 2"to 4" crack to the right.

Pitch 2 5.6

f. If you dislike struggling, climb up and left of the crack before you move back into it. Tackle the crack head on if you prefer climbing closer to your protection. You'll need a 2"to 3" piece higher. If you used your only 2" to 3" piece here, then you'll need to place something else above your head and snag the larger piece to take with you.

g. If this is your first experience with a hand crack, then take the time to learn to love them—they're your friends. Cup your hands, bring your thumb across your palm and rotate your wrist to accomodate the crack's width! What could be more bomber than this?

h. If this is your first lead then you may want to belay here. It will allow you to re-rack, communicate better and rest.

i. Solid belay anchors on this large ledge are few and far between. A good option is the "nut thread" on the left just as you reach the ledge. Slide the "clipping" end of a large wired nut through the hole in the rock and clip in—a trick worth knowing!

Climb the third pitch or walk off left.

Pitch 3 5.7 ❀

j. Everyone should summit this route at least once in their lives. Grapple with the flake/roof above. A cunning knee lock keeps it from being more than 5.7 and allows you to place protection. In fact, you can wedge your legs behind the flake and sit comfortably on it while you survey the protection and the moves above (and the great view below).

k. The summit. A nice place for a celebratory picnic.

Descent: Scramble north about 70' to the large notch, staying slightly east and below the ridgetop. There's a 2-bolt rappel anchor in the notch (the rappel is short—about 50').

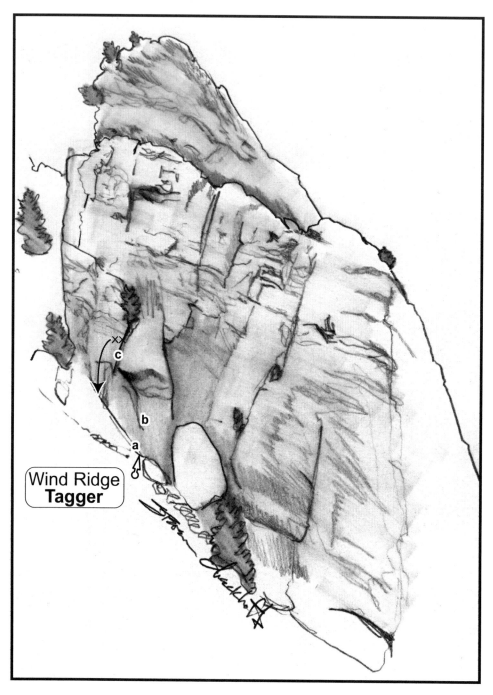

XX

c

b

a

Wind Ridge
Tagger

TAGGER - PITCH 1   5.9

This technical and insecure bit of climbing requires a great amount of poise and tenacity.

a. Stop here to place small cams, protecting several committing moves up to a stance on the face above.

b. Stop at this stance to place several wired stoppers and/or small cams which protect the committing moves up to and beneath the roof. The crux involves a double-dynosmear into a flying chickenwing. Just kidding . . . sort of! Once you're perched beneath the roof it's possible, though strenuous, to place gear (It's hard to see into the crack!).

c. Belay/rappel from two bolts. The second pitch, which climbs the slabby face into the dihedral capped by a 5.10 roof, is beyond the parameters of this book.

Descent: From the bolts, rappel 75' to the base.

The Wind Tower
Calypso 5.6

CALYPSO 5.6

This beguiling line is both immensely popular and deceptively serious, especially for beginning 5.6 leaders. A cavalier attitude on the first pitch has led to several accidents which were, in turn, the impetus for writing this book. It is, nonetheless, an exceptional climb. Calypso iseasily identified as the corner just left of the large boulder which leans against the wall.

Pitch 1   5.6 ⬤

There are four choices for gaining the crack, all of them hard to protect:

a. Traverse in from the left—delicate 5.5 on good, flat edges; or . . .

b. Go straight up—a slippery 5.9; or . . .

c. Chimney up the dihedral—charming but unprotected 5.6; or . . .

d. Step in from the right, after climbing the front of the leaning block; 5.5 ❖.

e. Upon reaching the crack you can place a small wired stopper and/or a cam of roughly 1.25".

f. Don't forget to use slings where necessary to alleviate rope drag.

g. Place several good pieces of protection beneath the roof as you move out right, including a 0.75" to 1" cam. Be prepared to climb 10' before getting your next protection in.

h. Treat this large flake gently.

i. Place a good piece in this 2"to 3" crack before casting out on the slippery traverse.

j. Gracious leaders always protect traverses for their seconds, not to mention themselves. This part of the pitch—with its surprisingly slopey holds and polished rock—has been the scene of several fatal accidents. A large cam here is de riguer!

You can make a 100-foot rappel to the ground from the bolts at the end of this pitch—be sure you have a 200' rope, or else use two ropes. However, if you do rappel you will miss out on some great climbing up above.

Pitch 2   5.6 ⚘

k. The excellent pro on this section allows you to savor the thrillingly steep and positive climbing. In a case like this, if one piece is good then two is better!

l. Place small wired nuts from this comfortable stance.

m. There is a welcoming "walk-off" ledge at the end of this pitch, below which you'll find your best anchor placements. Belay just below this ledge with your anchors behind you. Many people end the route here and avoid the final pitches, which are loose and wandering. If you want to escape on the walk-off ledge, see the descent notes on the following page.

Note: When bringing up your second, it's always a good idea to place your anchors behind and slightly above you, aligned with the vector of any potential fall, so that if your second suddenly leaps off the rock, you will not be violently yanked from your stance. Cinch the rope up snug between yourself and the anchors, so you cannot be pulled forward. If you do find yourself belaying from the ledge keep your weight very low to prevent toppling over the edge.

Pitch 3   5.4 🌸

n. Follow the path of least resistance over the bulge and belay at the tree.

Pitch 4   5.5 🌸

o. Weave your way up the ridge to the summit. The rock is suspect at times as is the protection, so tread lightly . . . .

Descent: From the summit, scramble north about 70' to the large notch, staying slightly east and below the ridge top. Reach a 2-bolt rappel anchor in the notch (the rappel is short, about 50').

From the end of pitch 2 you can escape either leftwards or rightwards along the large but exposed ledge. It is probably quicker and definitely simpler to take the left option.

The left option: traverse left on the walk-off ledge (5.2 R) past the arete of Wind Ridge, after which the ledge system angles down more easily into the gully.

The right option: traverse down and right to a 2-bolt rappel anchor on the wall above the ledge (this is just above Recon). The rappel from here is about 80' to a ledge system. From here you need to scramble up and left along the ledge to gain the two bolts atop the first pitch of Calypso, from which a 100' rap reaches the ground. If other climbers are on Calypso (and they most likely will be!) it is definitely worth avoiding this option.

Note: In exposed down-climbing situations such as you encounter on the various escapes from the Wind Tower, it's customary for the more experienced climber to belay their partner down first (the less-experienced party places protection as they go, thus protecting the second climber's descent as well).

Loose Rock

Entering the climbing environment with only a vague sense of the risks involved may leave you feeling helpless. It is, therefore, paramount that you develop the ability to perceive specific risks and duly respond to them. Loose rock is one risk associated with climbing. Reading about accidents resulting from loose rock and studying loose rock while bouldering will help you to avoid catastrophe.

All cliffs have loose rock, whether at the base, on the routes themselves or at the top. I have tried to choose climbs for this book that are well-traveled and have minimal loose rock. However, holds can and do break, even on trade routes. It is impossible to give advice on how to deal with loose rock in every situation. I can only recommend constant vigilance and ask climbers who dislodge a rock or drop gear to scream "ROCK!" so that others below can scramble to safety.

If a loose hold is an integral part of your climbing sequence, then you'll have to decide if you can use it without pulling it off (see illustration). Think not only about the consequences of a fall but also the path of the rock and who it might hit. Can you avoid using the hold? If not, you may want to consider backing down . . . .

Most loose flakes can tolerate some downward pressure but may give under outward pressure (pull down, not out). Check a dubious hold by rapping your knuckles against it; thump your fist (gently at first) against larger flakes and blocks. You'll soon develop an ear for more hollow or poorly-attached features.

Loose holds are but one danger. In a situation where the rope might dislodge loose rock it's essential that you redirect the rope in a safer line by running it through gear. Sometimes the only protection available is in less-than-desirable rock. The dilemma here is that a fall on the gear may dislodge the very rock in which it's placed. In many cases, the risk of chopping your rope or braining yourself or your partner will outweigh the psychological benefit of the protection.

With flexing flakes, aid climbers typically opt for cams over nuts because cams can hold body weight despite the give of the rock. Nonetheless, a large fall on a cam converts the downward force into outward force. As such, a camming device is not always your best choice when free-climbing expanding flakes. Though it may not hold as well, a stopper may be less likely to sheer away the rock. In some instances, slings may offer the best protection, as they tend to put less outward force on a flake or block and are therefore less likely to pull it off.

And finally: Climbers above you might knock something off and not even be polite enough to yell "Rock!" Consider wearing a helmet.

How to pull on loose and flexible holds — if you must.

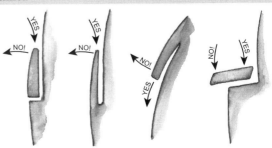

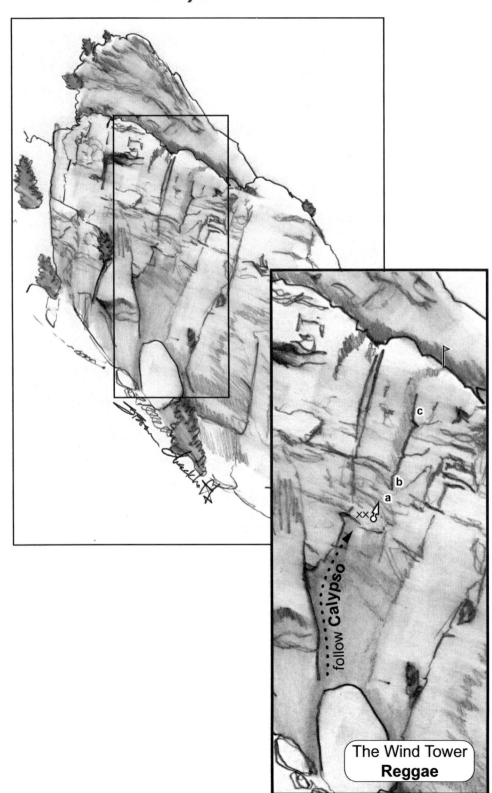

The Wind Tower
Reggae

follow Calypso

REGGAE 5.8

Reggae is the beautiful right-facing dihedral just right of Calypso's second pitch. This steep red corner is a common goal of parties who arrive at the ledge.

a. There are a couple of choices here. I sneak around to the right.

b. Place protection in the corner but be alert for face holds on the right.

c. There is an excellent knee lock where you join up with the wide crack. With your left foot on top of the flake rotate your hip rightwards and slide your knee into the crack. This slightly gymnastic maneuver takes weight off your arms. Practice this maneuver whenever possible—it will soon become a natural part of your "resting" repertoire.

Belay behind the large flake. Finish the route up one of the variations described in the notes for Calypso.

Descent: From the summit, scramble north about 70' to the large notch, staying slightly east of and below the ridge top. There's a 2-bolt rappel anchor in the notch (the rappel is short—about 50').

Three other routes on the west face of Wind Tower are suitable for aspiring leaders. They are marked on the topo on page 58. It is possible to rappel from the Calypso anchors to the ground (100') after the first pitch of each of these routes. These pitches are good, but are somewhat challenging first leads for their grade.

Recon: The first pitch is 5.2 if you exit the initial corner on the right.

The Bomb: The first pitch is 5.4.

West Overhang: The tricky first pitch is 5.7.

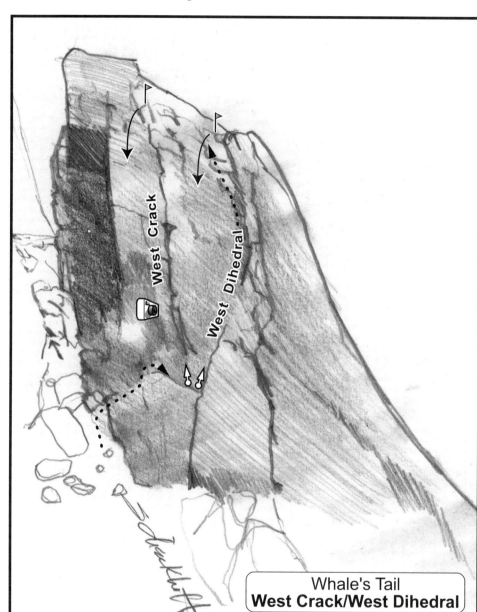

Whale's Tail
West Crack/West Dihedral

The Whale's Tail

Though this diminutive formation is studded with routes, there are three in particular that are popular with novice climbers and beginning leaders. They are: West Crack, West Dihedral and Clementine.

WEST CRACK 5.2

Traverse in from the left to reach the large ledge where this climb starts. The traverse in is nearly as hard as the climb itself. Most parties rope up for this "approach" pitch. This is also an excellent opportunity to practice leading traverses. Make sure that your placements are multi-directional so that the second, as well as the leader, benefits from the gear. The base of the actual West Crack is best reached by climbing from the obvious starting ledge to the next one up, moving right, then down-climbing through a wide crack in a large boulder to a comfortable ledge.

Pitch 1. The crack above is pure fun—it offers a variety of jam sizes and face holds. Additionally, it's about as easy to protect as anything you'll ever encounter.

Descent: A single-rope rappel from the fixed cable a little below the summit, back to the base of the route.

WEST DIHEDRAL 5.4

This fine pitch begins from the same large ledge as West Crack.

Pitch 1. Follow the path of least resistance up the fun corner which, like West Crack, is easily protected. Include some larger pieces (up to 4") for the crux near the top. Belay just above the dihedral, next to a fixed cable. You should place some gear above you so a falling second will not pull you from the stance. You can also climb a little further up and left to join West Crack, and belay there at its fixed cable. Place directionals if you decide to use this anchor.

Descent: A single-rope rappel from the fixed cable just to your left, back to the base of the route.

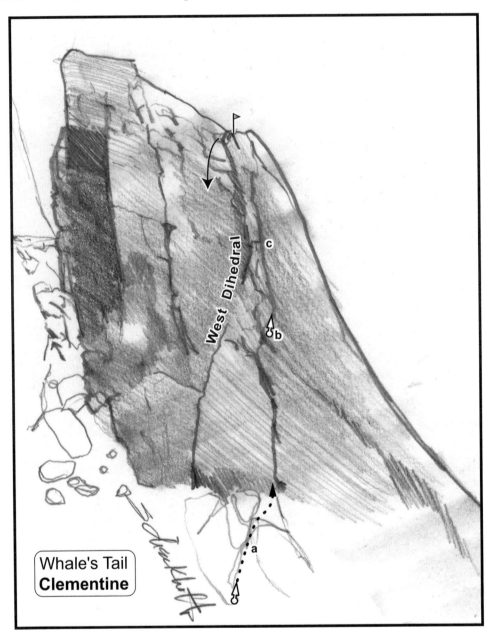

West Dihedral

c

b

a

Whale's Tail
Clementine

CLEMENTINE 5.5

Pitch 1   5.5 ⚸

a. Follow the crack and corner as shown in the topo.

Alternatively, you can simply scramble to the top of this pitch from the large ledge to the left. This (the way Clementine was originally climbed) is still the most popular means of accessing the arete above.

b. Belay on a ledge about halfway up.

Pitch 2   5.4 ⚸

c. The second pitch follows the spectacularly-situated arete. It's climbed most easily by first facing one way and then the other (I'll leave it to you to decide which is which). Belay as for West Dihedral; if the anchor's in use, ask the other party if they wouldn't mind sharing.

Descent: Rappel as for West Dihedral.

Laurie Beebe on West Crack
photo: Fran Bagenal

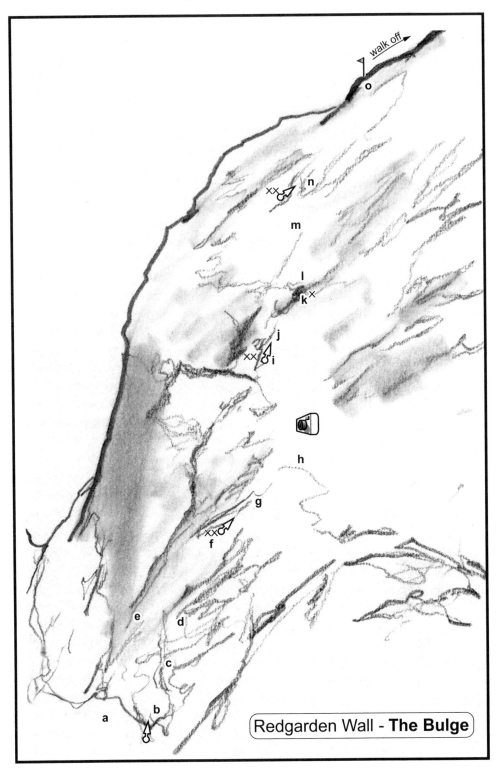

Redgarden Wall - **The Bulge**

Redgarden Wall

The Redgarden Wall dominates the skyline of Eldorado Canyon. It is a large complex mass of stone, featuring many of Eldorado's most sought-after routes.

THE BULGE 5.7

This climb, done in 1957, is a true period piece. The line, a bold jaunt over wavy rock that follows no crack system and has deliberately-placed fixed pro supplementing natural gear, is more characteristic of climbs done contemporaneously in The Garden of the Gods. First ascensionist Layton Kor rapped in after leading this climb to add the bolt on the crux third pitch. The aspiring Bulge leader must find solace in self-discipline, not the rope; much of the "easier" climbing on this line is undeniably runout.

You shouldn't tackle this challenging route until you're confident that you can climb 5.7 calmly, on your first try. I use the word "calmly" because it is crucial that you remain calm when faced with a myriad of route-finding choices—none of which involve lobbing off. On the positive side, the rock on The Bulge is very solid; the angle of the wall allows you to stand comfortably on your feet; and there are more holds than you'll know what to do with.

Pitch 1   5.6 ❀

a. The route is best approached from the east via the Wind Tower approach trail. From near the Wind tower's northern terminus (Wind Ridge) head west to the saddle between the Whale's Tail and the Redgarden Wall. A short scramble up a boulder leads to the base. The Bulge may also be reached from the west by scrambling up talus above the concrete slab.

b. Begin at the bottom of an interesting slab below a left-leaning groove. Trend toward the groove, keeep an eye out for small cam and stopper placements. Climbing over the rooflet is also pleasant.

c. At some point you'll tackle a sequence of 5.6 moves to gain a sloping shelf; the path you take is a matter of personal taste and mantling ability.

d. Once at the long, sloping shelf you have several choices for continuing over the bulge above. There is a fixed pin at the left end of the options.

e. Note that the shelf continues for about 50' to the left. It's possible to traverse this shelf but, owing to a steep move at the left end, it's better done left-to-right than right-to-left.

f. Belay at two bolts.

Pitch 2   5.5 ❀

g. Follow the diagonaling crack up and right past a few fixed pins (back these up with natural pro). The easiest sequence through here doesn't use the crack alone but parallels beneath it.

h. From the end of the crack follow an angling shelf system up and left. Though this 5.4 section is lower-angle than the traverse below, it's unprotected unless you can drape a sling over a knob and weight it so it doesn't lift off.

h. From the end of the crack follow an angling shelf system up and left. Though this 5.4 section is lower-angle than the traverse below, it's unprotected unless you can drape a sling over a knob and weight it so it doesn't lift off.

i. Belay at fixed anchors. If you rappel from here (two 50m ropes required) remember to tie a knot in both ends of the rope.

Pitch 3   5.7 ⚜

j. Follow a line of holds up and right. You can get some natural protection just above the belay but, once again, the easiest climbing is on the lower-angled face below and to the right.

k. About 25' up, a line of holds leads to the left below "The Bulge" proper. Follow these to Kor's bolt and make a very exposed step around and left (5.7).

l. Place a large cam above the crux traverse to protect your second. It's not an obvious placement, but your second will appreciate the gesture.

m. Weave up and left through an overlap then cruise up the face above to a belay niche.

Pitch 4   5.6 ⚜

n. Follow the line of least resistance (and least protection) up and right (5.6). Or if you're feeling ambitious, chug straight up the steep but juggy crack directly above the belay (5.9-).

o. After trending right you may need to angle up and left on the lower-angled slab to place an anchor in a thin crack/flake.

Descent: From this point most parties unrope and scramble about 100' north across exposed and risky 5.2 slabs to join a large gully system that leads up and right to a big, grassy ledge with several trees. You should consider staying roped-up until you get to the ledge. From here downclimb through the obvious notch to the north via 30' of 5.3. (This section is generally iced-up in winter months and may require a rappel). This drops you into the major gully system between Redgarden Wall and Hawk-Eagle Ridge. Wind carefully down this trail, downclimbing past a large chockstone in a constriction, until you rejoin the Wind Tower Trail.

Bob Barron on the second pitch of The Bulge. Note the sling around the knob to Bob's right.

Susan Schima on the dicey step-across move of C'est la Vie

Redgarden Wall
C'est la Vie

C'est la Vie with the Arete variation 5.9

This beautiful pitch has it all: clean rock, an aesthetic position, a good sunny exposition and a series of technical challenges. Though most parties lower from the first set of bolts, I recommend that you continue upwards to complete the full pitch. The route begins from a comfortable ledge fifteen feet above the scree field. Approach by heading straight up the talus directly above the cement slab.

Note the various descent possibilities and the rope requirements for each.

a. Make a long reach to sink your protection for the first moves. Test your piece from below (to do this, step down to the ledge, grab the rope running through the piece, pull it tight onto your harness so you can lift your legs off the ground, and jump up and down on it). If the piece pulls while doing this, the results should be embarrassing rather than injurious. Since this pitch begins from a ledge, you may wish to be "spotted" by an anchored person.

b. Place a cam to back up the fixed pin which, though it has held for decades, inspires little confidence during the awkward sequence it protects.

c. This undercling will force you to use good layback technique. Be strong, have faith and don't get your feet tangled in the rope!

d. Remember to use long runners as needed to mitigate rope drag.

e. Exit gracefully and enjoy the route's position. If you're heading for the anchor in the corner (**g**) take the low road. If not, get your RPs ready.

f. Tiptoe up the slab near the arete and by extending your reach with your nut tool you can slot a good nut high overhead.

g. The traverse to the belay at the base of the dihedral is quite airy and tenuous. You must trust your feet and move assuredly to reach the large holds. It is possible to rappel from the double bolt anchor with a 50-meter rope.

h. This belay is also an option if, for example, it starts to rain.

i. This somewhat uncomfortable, semi-hanging belay has a good line-of-sight with the upper part of the pitch and allows you to do an easy two-rappel descent via **g** or **h**.

j. A more comfortable belay stance here gives you a good line-of-sight with the ground but not with your partner.

Descent: The 150' rappel from here is most easily done with two ropes. If you have one rope, you can still get down, but you will need to do two shorter rappels, stopping at the intermediate "g" or "h" stations.

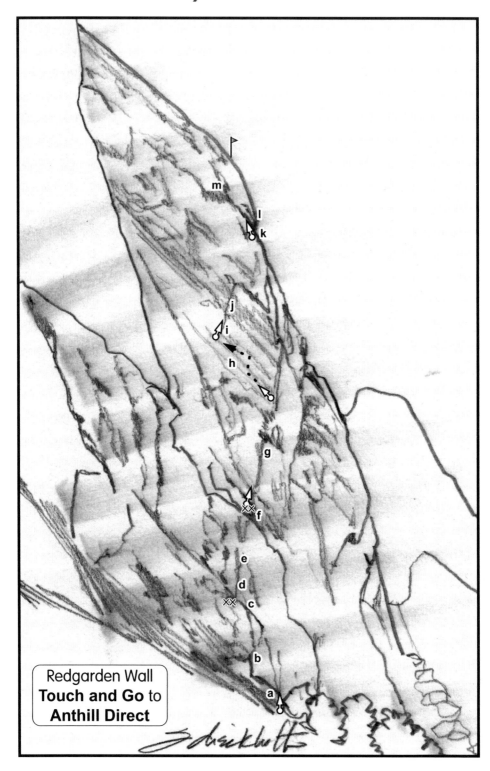

Redgarden Wall
Touch and Go to
Anthill Direct

TOUCH AND GO TO ANTHILL DIRECT 5.8

This link-up is the best route of its grade in Boulder, particularly if you take the 5.9 variation on the last pitch. The pitches are varied and aesthetic and the rock quality is optimal. Touch and Go starts at the east end of the long roof that runs diagonally across the south face of the Redgarden Wall. A small spring at the base leaves the staging area perpetually soggy.

Pitch 1   5.8+ ♣

a. Don't forget to thread a sling through the hole before you lurch upwards through the overhang, as a few messy ground-falls have occurred here.

b. This is an expanding flake, and while placing a nut in the bottom of it may seem like a good idea, you may never get the piece out. A cam may work better as would a higher nut placement.

c. It has become common practice to belay on this ledge. The most comfortable belay is at the spot marked "c" but one may also belay from two bolts further to the left.

d. Here's a chance to practice placing tiny wired nuts. This is a situation where you shouldn't fall—at least not until you get the larger piece in. Footwork and balance is as important as finger strength here.

e. Don't just fixate on what's in front of your face—feel around and you might be pleasantly surprised!

f. At the top of this pitch, belay from two bolts. If need be, these provide a rapid escape via a 130' rappel (two ropes) to the ground.

Pitch 2   5.8 ♣

g. If not for the initial bulge and the lack of decent pro on the slab this pitch would get a ☠ rating. The slab climbing is not quite hard enough to earn this pitch an **R**, but it is necessary to be good on your feet.

Pitch 3   5.6 R ◉

h. Your goal is a sloping ledge about 100' feet up and left; getting there demands good, patient route-finding. On runout terrain like this you should approach the climbing as an exercise in bouldering between stances. Deliberately consider each choice and exercise your ability to down-climb to a good stance before blindly "going for it." By this point in your career you should be able to execute 5.6 boulder problems with monotonous regularity.

i. Exercise your ropework skills by making use of the crack above when setting up your anchor.

Pitch 4   5.7 ☠

j. Angle up the thin crack, taking full advantage of the naturally-sculpted footholds on the right.

Pitch 5   5.9 ❀

k. There are a couple of ways to reach the obvious crack splitting the large bulge above. The location of your belay will affect your choice of paths.

l. Once at the crack you'll be able to toy with your protection before taking on this dramatically steep and exposed chimney/lieback (5.9).

m.The original last pitch traverses left from the belay (5.5+ ❀) before angling up sparsely-protected but easy slabs.

Descent: Follow the East Slabs descent, by angling down to an obvious large ledge with trees (see The Bulge descent section, page 70).

Note: This route is generally closed for raptor nesting from February 1 through July 31.

For long routes like this, it is often wise to study comprehensive guidebooks to look for escape routes in the event of bad weather. In this case, Psuedo Sidetrack may offer a quick escape from pitch 2.

Kath Pyke leading the Ruper Traverse   photo: Andy Donson

End to Another Great Day....

The Knowledge You Expect....
The Advice You Trust....

MOUNTAIN MISER

Denver's Climbing Authority

www.mountainmiser.com

Redgarden Wall
Ruper

RUPER 5.8

This long route combines great position with a myriad of climbing techniques.

Approaches:

1. Most parties approach via the slippery Lower Ramp (5.4 via the easiest path) but there are other more convenient alternatives.

2. Hike around to the west face of the Redgarden Wall and walk right (south) on the Vertigo ledge (20' lower than the Yellow Spur ledge) to its end. Belay across a downward traverse (5.5, exposed, and with a couple of loose blocks) that leads to the ledge at the start of Ruper. You will need to send the less experienced person first; they can place gear to protect the pitch for the "second." This allows you to leave packs on the Vertigo ledge and return to them via a simple rappel from the notch at the top of the Upper Ramp.

3. A third option is to climb the West Face of the Lower Ramp (5.2). This single pitch is perhaps the easiest and safest option for approaching Ruper. Hike up the West Face of Redgarden Trail until just past the cut-off for Kloof Alcove. Locate the start of this pitch about thirty feet left of a large Douglas Fir. Climb up to a large slabby ledge, and then head up and right into a recess. Aim for a large tree on the top of the Lower Ramp. This tree (usually equipped with slings) is also a great a rappel anchor if you need to make a rapid retreat from the top of the Lower Ramp.

Pitch 1   5.8 ❖

a. You can weave your way right through the slot before heading another 15' right. From here move left then up a ramp (5.4).

b. This short, right-facing corner is rather strenuous for a move or two.

c. This belay offers a good line-of-sight both above and below you. Spend some extra time setting up an anchor that's good for both upward and downward pull.

Pitch 2   5.8 ❖

d. This is the notorious Ruper Crack. You'll need some big (4") pieces to protect the lower part.

e. When the crack widens, you'll encounter an expanding flake inside the crack. Treat it gently, as it's the only way to protect this short section. Remember that when laybacking a wide crack you can often lever a leg into the crack, taking weight off your arms. A very slender person could even climb inside!

Pitch 3   5.7+ ❖

f. This is the famous Ruper Traverse. The crux moves are wildly exposed; memories of this unique, exciting position will stay with you. The leader has a virtual toprope but must remember to place protection for the second.

g. There is a suspect block here, but it can easily be avoided. You're now on the Upper Ramp, from which there are various means of escape. If you choose to descend, there are three main rappels:

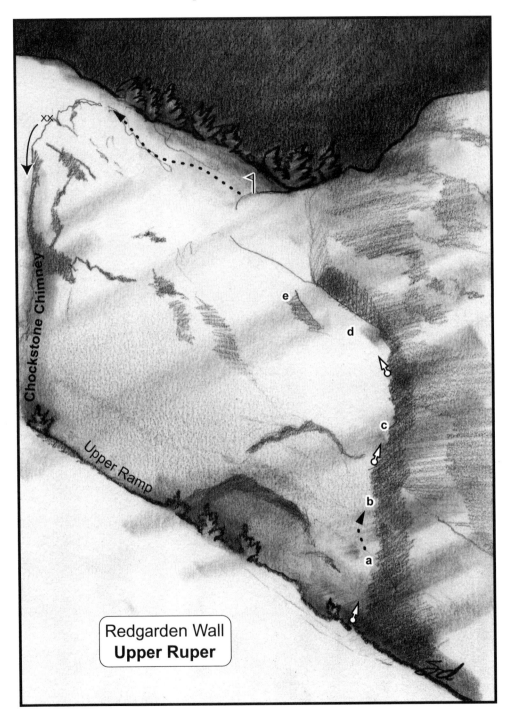

XX

Chockstone Chimney

Upper Ramp

e

d

c

b

a

Redgarden Wall
Upper Ruper

Descents from the Upper Ramp:

1) The best rappel route starts at a large tree wrapped in slings a short way down and west from the notch at the top of the Upper Ramp. Two single-rope rappels—60 feet to a pair of bolts, and then 80 feet to the ground—will get you back to Vertigo Ledge.

2) Hike gingerly down to the lower end of the Upper Ramp (be ultra-careful of loose rock through here, as anything you cut loose will go spinning off into the highly-trafficked areas below) and scramble around the corner (exposed 5.3). Three single-rope rappels (with two-bolt stations) from the base of the Naked Edge will get you back to the ground (the bolt anchors are not exactly directly under each other—don't rap past them).

3) From the top of pitch three of Ruper you can rappel from the tree or from a 2-bolt anchor 20 or so feet down and right. This double-rope rappel drops you at the start of Rosy Crucifixion, a short distance from "a" on Ruper's pitch one. From here, rappel to the Lower Ramp from an exposed sling anchor. Once on the Lower Ramp, you should belay or rappel down to the ground.

2 and 3 are not the primary rappel routes, but I do recommend that you know of them in case of an emergency.

Time and energy permitting, take on the fabulous Upper Ruper. These three pitches, up the inviting left-facing dihedral above, are more face-climbing intensive than the lower ones. Pitch 6 features a memorable traverse past some miserable pitons.

Pitch 4   5.7 ☸

a. Follow the large left-facing corner for about 30' then angle up and left. This moderately difficult section is rather runout. Stay calm.

b. Move back into the corner when convenient, then head around a roof to the left (5.5) and find a belay anchor.

Pitch 5   5.6 ⚛

c. Follow the dihedral and belay beneath the large roof.

Pitch 6   5.8 ☸

d. Make a 5.8 traverse left below the roof past a smattering of manky old pins then head up easier terrain to the saddle. The climbing after the traverse is generally below 5.6, but the holds are sometimes sloper. A careful leader will find protection.

e. The further you trend left, the easier the climbing. As always, protect the second on traverses.

As you may have gathered from the description, the protection on Upper Ruper is not as good as that on the lower pitches. Whoever leads pitches 4 and 6 should be confident on necky, runout climbing. Though, as Churchill once said, "Wager more than you can afford to lose and you will quickly learn the game," keep in mind that losing here can be permanent.

Descent: The descent is quite easy with two ropes: make a single rappel from double bolts down Chock-stone Chimney, a major left-facing chimney topping out roughly 150' to the west (left) of the top of Upper Ruper. This rappel can also be done with a single 60-meter rope. (Caution: a shorter rope won't reach the ground and you would have to downclimb the bottom) This gains the Upper Ramp. From here, use the descent description given in the "Descents from the Upper Ramp" section above. You can also descend via a long, exposed scramble down the East Slabs (see page 96).

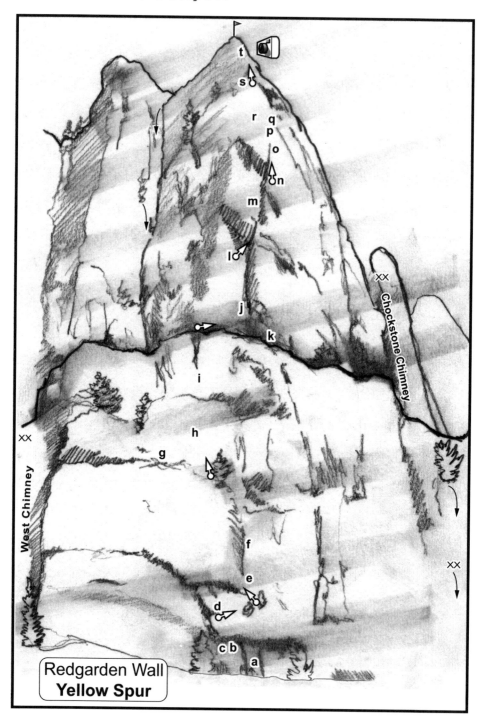

Redgarden Wall
Yellow Spur

West Chimney

Chockstone Chimney

THE YELLOW SPUR 5.9

This historic line weaves its way around and over a series of imposing features to reach an elegant solution. The last few pitches ascend a strikingly clean line up the simple yet graceful architecture of the final arete and pyramid-shaped summit. If the routes in this book are courses in composure then the quintessential Yellow Spur is a thesis on "grace under pressure." If, after doing many of the other routes in this book, you're able to climb Yellow Spur, you can rightfully consider yourself a good traditional climber.

Pitch 1   5.9

a. Begin in a short right-facing corner below a long roof (a 5.10c direct start is found 20' left but is outside the scope of this book). The difficulties in the corner start immediately. While spotted by your belayer, work in a small cam after the first move and a stopper just above that. Once established in the corner, you can fish in an RP or similar nut before reaching up to clip the old, fixed pin.

b. Remember to protect the traverse for your second.

c. Use long slings when clipping gear around the left end of the roof. You can back up the fixed pin with medium-sized gear.

d. Climbers usually belay at a small (and sadly now dead) tree 30' right, a set-up that creates rope-drag and communication problems with your partner. I recommend that you set up a belay on the ledge right above the overhang. You'll need to move your belay over to the tree below the second pitch unless you're using, and are proficient in the use of, double-ropes.

Pitch 2   5.8

e. Clamber carefully over the dead tree and traverse left on a rottenish band of purple rock to reach the bottom of a clean, right-facing corner.

f. Move right when the corner begins to seem too blank, even for Eldo!

Pitch 3   5.8

g. If you need to escape, a traverse up and left to a tree-covered ledge will afford you a fairly quick exit. From this ledge, one overhanging double-rope (165') rappel from a large tree gets you to the ground. If you have just one rope, continue left along the ledge for about forty more feet (exposed but fairly easy) to gain a bolt station atop the West Chimney. Two short raps from here (via a second bolt station) gain the ground.

h. Follow a thin crack through a short "tricky" section then motor up to a "rotten band."

i. Power-crawling into the V-slot is the crux. Take the time to place the best gear possible before heading up into these awkward moves.

Pitch 4   5.2 ❖

j. Traverse right (without knocking off any rocks) then head into the huge dihedral above. This pitch gets a ❖ rather than a ⚒ due to its thought-provoking nature for the grade.

k. Note: if you continue rightwards along the ledge you'll soon reach the top of the Upper Ramp, from which you can easily escape via the rappel route west of Vertigo (see *Descents from the Upper Ramp* page 81). Conversely, the ledge affords access to the upper part of Yellow Spur from the Upper Ramp, making link-ups with with routes like Ruper posssible. The ledge traverse is about 5.3.

Pitch 5   5.8+ ❖

l. An exciting hand traverse leads out right below a large roof. Don't overlook the gear placement afforded by a slot just above the main crack. This decreases the chance of your rope snagging on the lip of the roof.

m. Climb through another section of similar difficulty (5.8+) further up the corner.

n. Belay at an exposed stance on the arete ("The Perch"), anchoring yourself with good small stoppers and cams in the crack above you.

Pitch 6   5.9 ❖

o. Requiring good footwork and unfaltering tenacity, the Piton Ladder pitch marks a historic rite of passage. Show proper respect for those ancient pins by backing them up.

p. The large flake at the top of the thin crack should be handled with care. Clip the bolt above it with a long sling or two for a directional.

q. There is a subtle 5.10b direct finish on crimpers past the bolts above the flake.

r. Clever route-finding on the route's first free ascent led to the discovery of the Robbins Traverse, twenty unprotected feet of tricky 5.7. This sneaky leftward traverse still ranks as a thrilling, thought-provoking bit of climbing in an immensely exposed position.

s. Belay at a stance at the bottom of the final arete, taking care to avoid a nearby loose block.

Pitch 7   5.6 ❖

t. The transcendent summit pitch dances up a classic arete that is minimally protected but solid.

Descent: There are several ways to descend from the summit of T1:

1. The long slog down the East Slabs (see East Slabs Descent section, page 96). This requires adept route-finding lest you get "dead-ended" in one of the big gullies. This exposed excursion is made more hazardous by snowy or wet conditions and is best avoided in the event of an impending storm.

2. The Dirty Deed rappel route, used for decades, follows a line of trees west of the notch just behind and north of the summit. The first rappel anchor—a thread half hidden under a large block—is hard to spot owing to the fact that it is located in the notch. An 85' rap leads to a nice ledge with a large tree to the west (left) of the chimney. From here it is 105' to the large ledge below. An intermediate rappel can be found at a tree to the south (right) of the chimney. The lower section of this last rappel is fairly easy scrambling, which is a good thing, as the ropes usually hang up somewhere. This descent is direct, but don't be surprised if your rope gets get stuck or you pull down loose rocks. From the large ledge you can either scramble left (north) and rappel down the West Chimney (see notes for Pitch 3) or scramble down to a slightly lower ledge, then rap 165' down a steep, blank face from a tree.

3. The third option is to downclimb/scramble eastward from the notch (as for Descent #1) for about 400 feet until you can curve around south by some trees (this is near the top of Ruper) then west to a notch/ledge behind Italian Arete. From the far west end of this notch, rappel west to the top of the Upper Ramp from a big bolt anchor atop Chockstone Chimney, using either one 60-meter rope—be careful, this will just barely reach—or two ropes. Scramble 30 feet west to the top of the Upper Ramp, then down and west about 20' to a large tree with slings. Rappel from here 60' to a bolt anchor, then 80' to Vertigo Ledge, just south of the start of Yellow Spur. Though fast and safe, it takes a little route-finding to find Chockstone Chimney.

Crusher Bartlett on Yellow Spur. photo: Fran Bagenal

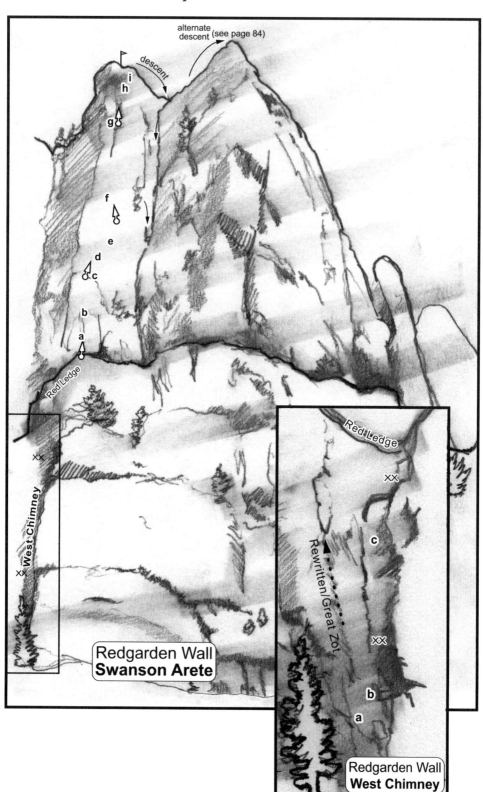

alternate descent (see page 84)

descent

i
h

g

f

e

d
c

b

a

Red Ledge

West Chimney

Redgarden Wall
Swanson Arete

Red Ledge

Rewritten/Great Zot

c

b

a

Redgarden Wall
West Chimney

WEST CHIMNEY/SWANSON ARETE 5.5

High on the west side of Redgarden Wall, the clean, sweeping line of the Swanson Arete draws the eye. Though you must battle up the unfriendly West Chimney to reach the Swanson Arete, it's well worth the price of admission!

Pitch 1 (West Chimney) 5.5 ❖

a. Begin to the left of the actual chimney and climb about 50' up a small corner.

b. Step right and tackle the main chimney which, despite its name, requires a minimum of actual chimneying.

c. Be aware of loose rock on and near Red Ledge, particularly since anything you cut loose will land in a popular staging area.

Red Ledge links many routes on the west side of Redgarden Wall, from Green Slab 200' left to The Yellow Spur 200' right.

Pitch 2 5.4 ⚲

This is the first pitch of Swanson Arete.

a. Climb parallel thin cracks up the wall directly below/slightly right of the crest of the arete.

b. Though there's loose rock here and there on this section, you can easily steer clear of it.

c. The best belay is near a tree in a short corner; other options are available as well.

Pitch 3 5.5 ❖

d. Climb up to and through a short slot, then make a sly downward traverse to the right.

e. Avoid excessive drag by paying attention to your ropework. Pull over the small bulge and belay.

Pitch 4 5.5 ⚲

f. The higher you go, the better the climbing! Follow the attractive crack system up the crest of the arete.

g. It will be easier to communicate with your partner if you belay near this tree.

Pitch 5 5.5 ⚲

h. Finesse your way up the dihedral then traverse right around the roof.

i. Step from an airy perch into the short corner leading to the summit. A small wired nut provides excellent protection for this move.

Descent: Downclimb south to the notch between Swanson Arete and Yellow Spur. It's a little tricky (5.4 or so) near the bottom, so you may want to stay roped up. From here, descend as for Yellow Spur (see Yellow Spur descent notes, page 84).

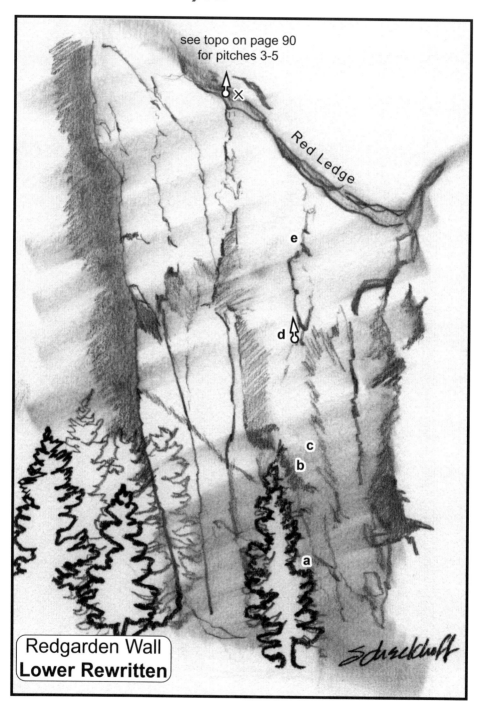

see topo on page 90
for pitches 3-5

Red Ledge

e

d

c

b

a

Redgarden Wall
Lower Rewritten

REWRITTEN 5.7

This route, a kinder, gentler version of Yellow Spur, has a spectacularly-situated upper half. I've provided directions for the first two pitches of Rewritten, but you should also consider the harder, but better-protected, first pitch of the adjacent Great Zot (see page 93).

Pitch 1   5.6 ⊛

a. From the base of the West Chimney follow a ramp up and left into a steep sequence. Since protection is sparse, make each piece count. Though the climbing requires good footwork, it isn't sustained.

b. Pull over a small bulge on the arete; this is probably the technical crux.

c. Traverse right to the Great Zot crack. This is a good opportunity to practice your 'cross-over' move.

d. Continue up the Great Zot crack and belay from a good stance behind a large flake at the base of a chimney.

Pitch 2   5.4 ⊛

e. Climb the chimney and face above to Red Ledge. The traverse left to a huge bolt on the ledge requires attentive ropework.

Pitch 3   5.5 ❖

f. Head straight up from the bolt belay then tiptoe delicately past some large blocks.

g. Swarm up a chimney and belay in the niche above.

Pitch 4   5.7 ❖

h. A beautiful hand-traverse leads left across the wall. The footwork on this traverse is challenging—you may find it harder than the crack above. Try heel-hooking!

i. After the hand-traverse, tackle the steep thin crack, which offers up both solid gear and user-friendly footholds.

j. Weave upwards to a great little belay stance in an airy position.

Pitch 5   5.6 ❖

k. Begin this elegant pitch by stepping up onto the right side of Rebuffat's Arete, which you follow for the first third of the pitch.

l. For the middle third of the pitch shift to the left side of the arete to find protection.

m. The last third finishes back right. Bring slings so you can loop horns for protection.

n. Follow the arete to a fantastic, photogenic stance at the Point.

o. If you choose not to belay at the "Point" then continue up the cracks (5.5) to the summit.

Descent: The easiest descent is via a walk-off to the north. From the summit spot a hard-to-see cairn on another summit about 500' north; this marks the top of an easy hike back down to the trail.

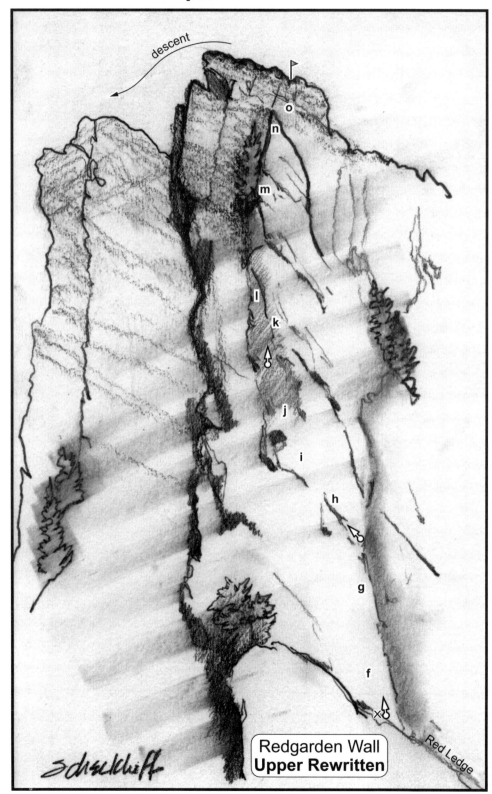

Redgarden Wall
Upper Rewritten

descent

o
n
m
l
k
j
i
h
g
f

Red Ledge

schackleff

Self-Rescue

As climbers, you and your partner are responsible for getting yourselves home safely. Although there are various agencies who provide some degree of rescue, your safety is primarily in your own hands. A knowledge of self-rescue and first-aid techniques should be part of your training. For example, prussic slings are easily brought along and are essential for both ascending the rope and tying off a fallen climber . . . Now, do *you* know how to use them?

You can best avoid accidents by honing your down-climbing skills, practicing good judgement about the weather and assessing dangerous rock-fall situations. In Colorado the weather can change quickly; know the direction it's coming from (usually the west) and learn to recognize the signs of an approaching storm.

Red Ledge

e

xx

d

xx

c

b

a

Redgarden Wall
Great Zot

schreckhoff

THE GREAT ZOT (TO RED LEDGE) 5.8

This splendid, well-protected route has become quite popular in recent years. Once at Red Ledge you can either rappel or carry on to other routes, making for great link-up potential.

Pitch 1   5.8

a. Left of the bottom of the West Chimney is a corner with a thin crack. Follow this to a sloping ledge (5.5) then move left to a recess. The West Chimney route typically follows this corner before stepping right.

b. Work up into the bulging, flared crack and place good protection, taking care to leave the best jams free for your hands. A few 5.8 moves get you through the crux.

c. Follow the finger and thin-hand crack (5.5) to a comfortable belay stance.

Pitch 2   5.4

d. If you wish to continue on the Swanson Arete or other routes to the right then follow the flake/shelf system rising up and right via a romp through sparsely-protected 5.2.

e. To either continue on Rewritten or rappel from the huge ring bolt on Red Ledge you'll need to work up the left-facing chimney to Red Ledge, which you follow left. Be extra careful on this pitch, which suffers from both a paucity of gear and a smattering of loose rock.

The rest of The Great Zot meanders up the large wall above, between Rewritten and the large corner . . .

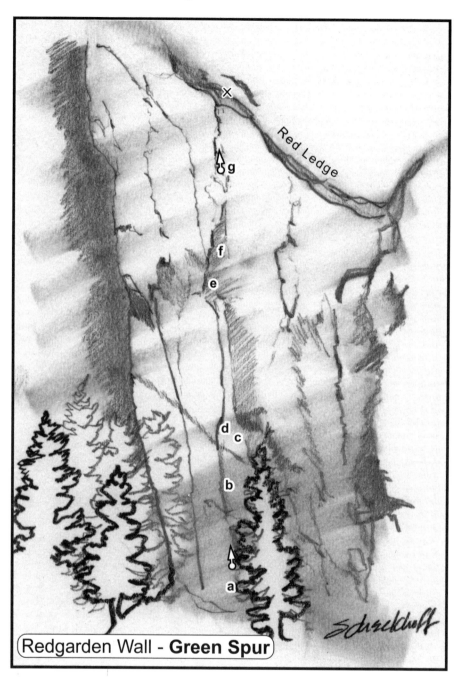

Redgarden Wall - **Green Spur**

Green Spur 5.9 (to Red Ledge)

This excellent west-facing crack line on the west side of Eldo's Redgarden Wall is not really spurious. The first long pitch seems to have a little of everything. This splitter line can be done in its entirety or linked up with several other good routes. You can also stop at Red Ledge, as described here, where you'll find a fixed rappel anchor.

Pitch 1 5.4

a. The fixed anchor mentioned above is unreachable with a 50-meter rope; it is best to scramble up to a small ledge. You can also continue up to the base of the chimney and belay there, making this pitch about 5.4.

Pitch 2 5.9

b. If you didn't belay at the base of the chimney, this will give you a chance to generate some momentum!

c. If you get spanked by the main line, the crack on the right goes at 5.8.

d. A rule of thumb about climbing offwidths and squeeze chimneys is to put your back on the "downhill"side (5.9).

e. Once at the steep corner you can rest, sink good gear and get psyched for the second 5.9 crux. Effective stemming will save you a lot of effort.

f. Look for a good foothold out right; step over when you can.

g. Though you can belay here, it's better to continue up to the huge bolt on Red Ledge.

Descent: Rappel from the huge eye-bolt. This requires double 60-meter ropes. Lacking these, scramble down and right to the top of the West Chimney where there is a bolt station. Two 80' raps from here (via a second bolt station) gain the ground.

The East Slab Descent

This exposed descent is most often used to get off routes in the vicinity of Anthill Direct, but can be used for all routes ending up on top of Redgarden Wall. It is a good way down if you'd rather not rappel or if the rappel routes are crowded.

If you have just completed one of the routes on the west face of Redgarden such as Yellow Spur, head down east into a wide boulder-choked gully. This empties out near Tower Two (near the top of Upper Ruper). Skirt north of this summit, out of the gully, then head down the slabs proper. About halfway down the East Slab notice a prominent, grassy ledge system with a few large trees (the ledge rises to a notch on its north end). To get to the notch head as far north on the East Slabs as you comfortably can—a couple of low-angle slots marked by small trees make this feasible. If you head too far south you'll end up at the bottom of the ledge system, which you must then follow up and north to the notch. From the notch downclimb a 30' slabby corner (5.3) to a climbers' trail in the vegetated gully north of Redgarden Wall. This corner stays iced-up in winter months and can be quite dangerous; if that is the case you should rappel.

Follow the climbers' trail down past a gravelly section to a large boulder/chockstone. The slot below is best down-climbed by backing into it! Solid handholds facilitate a reverse 5.2 layback into this body-length chimney. Though the rock is polished, you do have one good foothold inside to go for. If it's getting too dark to see, you might have to downclimb the slab. Sometimes this slab is wet at the bottom. The trail becomes easier to navigate past here. Stay close to the rock on your left (Hawk-Eagle Ridge) and traverse to the Wind Tower descent trail, a veritable super-highway.

Excuses

In his classic article entitled "The Art of Climbing Down Gracefully," legendary Scottish climber Tom Patey listed a variety of excuses for retreating from a climb, all of which avoided the brutally honest truth—"because I wasn't a good enough climber today." Much like the routes described in this book, I have tested these excuses myself and can vouch for their quality.

A popular excuse for slumping limply onto the rope, despite protection at your waist that would hold a truck, is to announce that the holds are "greasy." Most likely, the holds are "greasy" because of the dithering that's been going on; nevertheless, you can't be expected to climb on less-than-perfect holds. The downside to using this all-too-common excuse is that your partner may soon suspect the truth.

The "greasy holds" ploy is a variant on Patey's classic "The Chossy Climb," in which the climber's aesthetic sensibilities are so offended that he's incapable of continuing upward. Modern variations also include the "Bad Rock" excuse and the "Needs Cleaning" ploy.

Faking an injury is effective but can only be done so often—remember the little boy who cried wolf? Equally credible and quite fashionable (particularly in the People's Republic of Boulder) is to whine that you "haven't warmed up properly." You could have done the moves but didn't want to risk straining a precious tendon.

Patey also explains his crafty yet effective "Wrong Gear" excuse: "With a little foresight it is always an easy matter to bring the wrong equipment for the day, and then allow everyone to share your vexation." While he describes bringing ice gear for a rock climb or vice versa, it's easy to see how you could employ this at a Front Range crag. Conveniently "forget" to bring big gear for a wide crack or try the "Wrong Shoe" routine, a ploy which still smacks of the credible, despite advances in shoe technology. Simply announce that you're wearing a friction shoe on an edging climb and thus cannot continue. The sheer pathos of the moment will be enough to make grown men cry.

A final, last-ditch option is to give voice to that one unutterable truth—"I'm not a good enough climber today." Facing an injury (or worse) you choose to retreat and, perhaps, to try again another day. This excuse is used so rarely that only the most self-assured among us should consider it.

The West Ridge - **Long John Wall**

West Ridge

LONG JOHN WALL 5.8

Once above the first pitch, this fine route follows an engaging series of pleasantly-sized cracks. Its sunny exposition makes this a great route to try during cooler weather.

Pitch 1   5.6 🌀

a. Historically, the first pitch climbs up and traverses left into a leaning slot before tackling the short face above. If the poison ivy is blooming, there is an alternative route.

b. The alternative: Follow the right-facing corner until you can traverse right (5.4) and up.

c. In either case, you're faced with a step up into the two-move crux, which takes you to a ledge and the belay a short scramble higher. Place one nut at your feet and another in front of your face. Here's a good trick for keeping a nut rigged for downward force in place: Connect the nut to an "upward pull" placement beneath it then clip in with a separate sling. You can also weight the top piece with something like a full water-bottle and, once again, clip in with a separate sling.

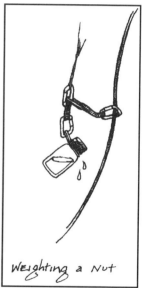

Weighting a Nut

Pitch 2   5.8 🦋

d. Climb blissfully up the crack until you can step left, then move up to a perch beneath the overhang.

e. If you've learned to love hand-jamming (see Wind Ridge), you'll be amazed at how easy this roof feels. Otherwise you're in for a world of hurt!

f. I prefer to belay next to the fixed pin. Back it up, of course.

Pitch 3   5.6 ❖

g. Loose rock abounds on this ledge. One of the virtues of belaying at the pin is that you can find shelter in case of falling rock. Leaders, take care not to flip any rocks down when trailing your rope across this ledge. At the left end of this ledge you can rappel (1/2 rope) to escape.

h. Head up the slot and belay, when possible, beneath the next bulging wall.

Pitch 4   5.8 🦋

i. Conquer the right-facing corner on the left via good jams and even better protection. If your fists are the size of your head you can keep jamming, otherwise you're better off laying it back!

j. Sometimes it's good to keep the pitch short in order to facilitate climber-belayer communication. Note the escape rappel possibility (1/2 rope) out left on this ledge.

Pitch 5   5.5   🪓 🪓

k. To the top!

Descent: There are two main options for returning to the base of the climb. Option A involves angling down across the loose slope to the trail near the west side of Redgarden Wall (facing you). Follow this trail down and around the toe of the West Ridge then retrace your steps back up the West Ridge Trail.

Option B is quicker but more adventurous. Work your way up the ridge on its east side past the next two "towers" (Sooberb and Handcracker) to find a west-angling walk-off. Some downclimbing is involved . . . if you find yourself on anything harder than 5.2 then you're in the wrong spot!

Once on the ground you'll be near the obvious juggy crack of Positively 4th Street and just uphill of the Pony Express area.

There are three worthy pitches on this sector of the West Ridge that I recommend for climbers learning to lead at these grades:

Positively 4th Street 5.9+

Pure pleasure, this short one-pitch route takes great gear! You can step left (5.8) at the top of the crack to avoid the final, crux move.

Descent: The descent is an easy walk off to the left.

Pony Express 5.9

The first pitch of Pony Express is a pleasant little pitch leading to a ledge with a tree and a pair of bolts just right. As you climb, keep your eyes peeled for face holds out right.

Mescaline 5.7+

This is a one-pitch route about 20' to the right of Pony Express. This leads to the same pair of bolts just right of the tree atop pitch one of Pony Express.

Descent: for both these pitches, an 80' rappel from the bolts just reaches the ground—be careful.

The Bastille
Werk Supp

The Bastille

Werk Supp 5.9+

The first pitch climbs a series of short flourishes that add up to a graceful whole. The second pitch is redoubtable and as uncompromising as a knife fight. Though most leaders thrive on the bold sweeping gestures of the first pitch, few return to join the fray on the second.

Pitch 1   5.8+   ❖

a. The first 30' of the climb is laced with variations; your objective is the finger crack that emerges from this confusion. The climbing tends to be easier on the left and harder (5.9) on the right, so stay left. The route follows a series of large flakes. Treat these flakes with caution despite the fact that they're caked in chalk and literally thousands of people before you have tugged on them.

b. At 50' you'll hit a couple of large blocky flakes; these too should be handled with care (pull down, not out!). Avoid sinking gear behind the separate "block-like" flakes, as there are quite solid straight-in cracks nearby. Don't forget to take advantage of the rest stance below the crux!

c. The first thing you'll notice about the crux is the excellent gear a step or two above the resting stance. The crux sequence is more easily tamed by balance and footwork than brute force.

d. You can get great gear in the crack above the crux. Another rest is coming up!

e. The only possible problem you face from here on out is running out of pro. Don't miss the rest you get by leaning into the corner to unweight your arms.

f. At the top of the crack there are two options. While well-protected, continuing up the crack is technically more difficult (5.8+). Stepping left takes you further away from your gear but goes at 5.6. If you go straight up, don't forget to protect your second.

g. Belay just left at double bolts on the long, sloping ledge. From here you can either continue up the second pitch or rappel (just one rope needed) to anchors atop a 60' pedestal down and to the east. Alternately, fire off a short pitch along the ledge to the right to connect with the Bastille Crack near the top of its second pitch. The traverse goes at 5.6+ and the crux 'step-around' can be protected with small gear.

Pitch 2   5.9+   ❖

h. Some of the terror induced by this pitch can be ameliorated by milking its perfect jams. Bring an adequate supply of 2" to 4" cams and be prepared for a major battle getting into the flare.

i. Though jamming lets you place excellent overhead protection, upward progress past this point may require cunning use of your peripheral vision.

j. Belay on a secure ledge above. The appealing short pitch above the belay is the last pitch of March of Dimes (5.10c).

Descent: The descent involves exposed scrambling around to the east (left), down a ramp, then over to a primitive trail. Don't head down too soon.

The Bastille
Bastille Crack

BASTILLE CRACK 5.8

This legendary route was put up by anonymous Army climbers in the mid-fifties. Due to its easy access, appealing length, purity of line, generally well-protected nature, flat, pleasant summit and easy descent route, Bastille Crack has become overwhelmingly popular. Regardless of the season, the Bastille Crack is certainly the most popular climb in Boulder. Its north-facing aspect makes it ideal on a hot summer day. On the other hand, the first pitch has been the scene of several nasty ground falls; parties are often forced to retreat for various reasons; and the crack often sports an ornamental array of stuck pieces.

From the anchors atop the first pitch you can easily toprope the Northcutt Start (5.10+), the left-facing corner left of the crack itself. As you may know, this route was the scene of a famous "sand-bagging" episode in 1959 when Ray Northcutt was told that the indomitable Layton Kor had free-climbed the pitch a day earlier. Not to be outdone, Northcutt freed the route using two pitons for protection in what was probably America's first 5.10 lead!

Pitch 1   5.8

This 65' pitch ends at a pair of bolts, from which some parties rappel. Carefully study this pitch before you head up. Several leaders have gotten into trouble here, due more to haste than anything else.

a. Fish in some good small gear before you step up to the left-facing flake, which also takes good pro. You must place good protection before taking on the leftward traverse into the main crack. Remember to use long slings to alleviate rope-drag.

b. The climbing quickly becomes strenuous in the main crack. Guess the size of the crack beforehand and have a pre-selected cam or nut clipped to a quickdraw and ready to go. If you can reach left and place a piece before committing yourself to the moves, all the better! In fact, you could even downclimb to the ground and test the piece (see C'est la Vie, page 73), a smart and impeccably stylish move!

c. Once established in the main crack get back in balance and work your hands into solid jams. Place your next piece; back it up if you have time. (Keep in mind that by placing more than one piece you risk plugging up the best jams.) Continue once you have good gear in.

Pitch 2   5.6

This next pitch follows the crack for nearly 100' to gain a large ledge system. It is possible to do these first two pitches in one, but you will regret it once you realize you will neither be able to see your second — nor hear them over the noise of the river.

d. Route-finding shouldn't be a problem on this pitch. This delightful romp allows you to climb up, over, around and through a crack, with good protection always within arm's reach. Be extra-careful when placing cams in the flared section, as they tend to get stuck.

e. Near the top, as the angle starts to ease back, step left out of the main crack (the lieback to the right is 5.8+) and follow nice holds up to a belay on a large, angling ledge beneath a double crack. If you need to escape you're best off rappelling and leaving gear for anchors.

Pitch 3   5.7 ⚔

f. Though steep, this short (50') pitch is both well-protected and blessed with great holds. As you set up for the moves, focus on good, precise foot placement and effective body position.

g. The crux (if you could truly call it that) comes at the top in the double cracks. Belay immediately above here. Should you need to descend from here (due to a thunderstorm, for example), your best option is to rappel (from your own gear) the large sloping ledge eastwards to the bolt anchors for Werk Supp and March of Dimes, which are about 60' below you.

Pitch 4   5.7 ❖

h. Traverse left and slightly downward to a blocky corner. This is a "classic" rope-drag situation—use long slings on most, if not all, of your pieces. The climbing from niche to niche can be awkward in spots.

i. Weave your way up the broken corner to a belay on the slab above.

Pitch 5   5.4 or 5.8 ❖

j. The easiest alternative here is a 5.4 chimney on the left.

k. If you're still not pumped, fire up the rightmost corner by following a line of holds up its left wall. Along the way you'll find some fixed protection, which you can easily back up with solid placements of your own. Though the climbing gets more balancey the higher you go, there are good jams above and below the rooflet at the top.

Take some time to reward yourself with the stellar view of Redgarden Wall and the rest of Eldo from this airy, flat summit.

Descent: work southwards along the prominent ledge system on the west side of the Bastille to the Fowler Trail. Be careful on the ledge system—some sections are very exposed. From where you hit the Fowler Trail, head straight down the talus on the west side of the Bastille, close to the cliff, on a climber's trail which becomes better defined as you go lower.

At the beginning of the traverse on the ledge system you'll see the remnants of an old high-wire anchor. These venerable cables once anchored Ivy Baldwin's high-wire, spanning 635 feet to Wind Tower and crossing a good 582 feet above the canyon floor. Amazingly, Baldwin made the trip eighty-nine times before his eighty-second birthday. His wife put a halt to further crossings when she threatened to shoot the stabilizing sandbags with a rifle if he attempted to walk again.

Communication

Traditional climbing fosters and requires a close communication with your partner. Before a climb partners should assess the route, descent and the weather. Constant attention must be given to belaying and rope-handling and you and your partner need to be clear and concise in the signals you use.

On belay, climbing, off belay, ROCK! and *slack* are the commonly used verbal signals. When you are belaying and cannot see your partner you have to cultivate a refined sense of their movement. Too much tension on the rope could pull them off balance and of course too much slack may allow a more dangerous fall. Just as the belayer needs to be attentive the climber needs to be patient. Don't lose your composure.

Often there are environmental impediments (wind, traffic, streams, and other people for example) to clear communication so try to anticipate them and make allowances. On a spring day in Eldo when the creek is raging, most verbal signals sound alike. You may find hand signals useful. In addition I've shortened the recommended pitch lengths occasionally in this book in order to keep the partners in visual contact; you should keep this in mind when using other books. While some climbers use rope signals (light tugs), this can create its own obvious problems. A good safe alternative is for the leader to pull up all the slack through the belay device rather than pulling it up hand over hand. The second can then rest assured that he is on belay when the rope comes tight. This eliminates second guessing on verbal signals, hand jestures, or rope tugs.

I SEEM to BE LOSING MY GRIP.

what? you're thinking of taking a trip? it's so expensive

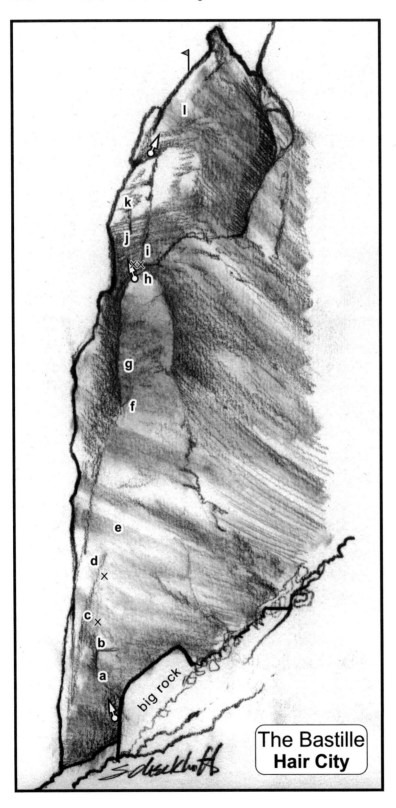

The Bastille
Hair City

HAIR CITY 5.9R

This is one of the few routes in the book that involves climbing above gear on terrain that's nearly as hard as the crux itself. Hair City is a clean, striking line, as rewarding as it is bold. Its elegant sequences on good, crisp edges will have you coming back for more!

Pitch 1   5.9 ☺

a. Begin from the first terraced landing on the Bastille descent trail. Climb up a body-length crack. Step left into a short right-facing corner with a fixed pin. As with most fixed pins, you should back this one up!

b. Mantling onto the narrow ledge is awkward (I stylishly use my knee); fortunately, it's fairly easy to reverse back down to the rest between attempts.

c. After solving the problem and clipping the first bolt, pull up and left until you're standing in balance on good holds. Remember to relax and trust your feet.

d. Just above the second bolt is a thin move to good holds. There are a couple of solutions here. The most practical path is to step left then climb up to a good rest. The direct line punches straight up past an excellent nut placement.

e. In either case, you'll need to traverse right to reach a virtual bucket-ladder. This section is runout! Be sure of your protection before you commit to the "bucket ladder." The balancey 5.7 climbing through here demands attentive sequencing; as with chess, plan a move or two ahead.

f. Clamber up to a stance below the bulge at the bottom of the big flake, where you'll find one perfect nut placement and several also-rans. You can also fish in an RP up and right in the bulge. Though the rock here is somewhat suspect, the RP is worth placing nonetheless.

g. After a long pull over the bulge there is a placement for a large nut. I prefer to traverse left with my feet at the lip here and get to good holds soon rather than flirt with the balancey moves higher. In either case, a fall would be bad.

h. Belay at the top of the huge block/flake. If you tie in with enough slack you can sit out on the edge of the block, providing a good view of your partner for most of the pitch. A double-rope rappel from the bolts will get you back to the ground. Make a quick check over the edge before you fling the ropes; it's difficult for people below you to hear a warning shout, and the rope-ends whip directly across the trail.

Pitch 2   5.9 ☺

i. Climb up to the "rotten band" ledge above and tie off a natural chockstone, which you can back up with a cam.

j. Step left and contemplate the bouldery sequence leading to the lip of the bulge/roof. Although the first hold is suspect, subsequent holds are positive and seem solid. Place a crucial 0.5" stopper at the lip of the bulge and work out the long reach above. Take care not to knock out the stopper as you pass.

k. The rest stance above is followed by sweet climbing on "boilerplate flakes" up the steep headwall. Your best bet is to sling the horns and flakes for protection! Belay on a nice ledge about 50 feet above the belay, keeping you in both voice and sight range of your second. You will both be grateful for this if your second has a struggle at the roof.

Pitch 3   5.5

l. Pull the bulge and angle up and right on more "boilerplate flakes" to a belay near the summit.

Descent: follow the same descent as for Bastille Crack (see page 106).

A low-gravity day at the office; Derek Hersey enjoying West Arete.
photo: Derek Hersey collection

Toproping

On high-gravity days, when neither you nor your partner is up to leading, hiking around to the top of the cliff and dropping the rope down an appealing line is a great way to keep climbing.

Toproping is a time-honored method of honing your skills on routes that you wouldn't be comfortable leading or bouldering out. Toproping has all the virtues of bouldering, with the added benefit that you gain a little altitude and get to work on your endurance.

Unfortunately, excessive toproping may lead to a psychological dependency on the security of the toprope. Climbers who limit themselves exclusively to seconding pitches or to leading only sport climbs (where all the protection is fixed) may develop a similar complex.

If you aspire to lead a particular route but lack the requisite confidence you can either set it up as a toprope, or better yet, persuade someone else to lead it. Seconding will allow you to practice all the moves and to remove the protection, thus providing a lesson in nutcraft and preparing you to lead it yourself.

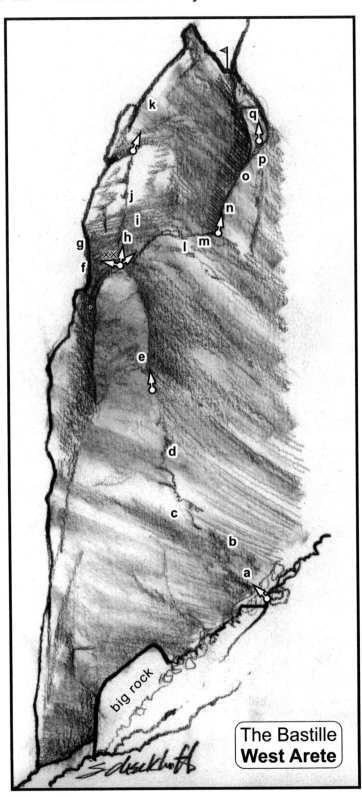

The Bastille
West Arete

WEST ARETE 5.8+

This elegant line can be linked with various other climbs en route to the top of the Bastille. The first ascent was free-soloed in 1984 by Duncan Ferguson.

Pitch 1   5.8+ ❖

a. Step off the second terrace on the Bastille descent trail. You'll gain instant exposure as you diagonal up and left (5.6) towards two small cracks below a longer, thin crack at roughly 40'.

b. Sink small pieces in both of the small cracks and make them count! The moves above are awkward and insecure on slick, diagonaling edges that may feel harder than their 5.8+ grade.

c. A one-inch slot on the left takes gear.

d. There's a little stance at the thin, vertical crack. The steep, pocketed wall above makes for an aesthetic, interesting crux. I recommend belaying on the ledge above to maintain good communication with your partner.

Pitch 2   5.6 ❖

e. Grovel into the chimney then worm your way to the top of the huge block/flake. Remember that in a chimney no one can see you struggle! Take care with the finishing moves to the huge block/ledge (where you'll find a two-bolt belay).

A double-rope rap from here will get you down. Don't throw the ropes down until you can see the ground and the rock beneath you. The ends of the ropes tend to lash the popular trail and climbs below. It's especially hard to get the attention of climbers below when creek noise is high.

There are four options for your summit bid from atop Pitch 2:

A. Pitch 3 of The West Buttress;

B. Pitches 3 and 4 of The West Face;

C. Pitches 3, 4 and 5 of The West Chimney;

D. Pitch 2 of Hair City (see Hair City section on page 109 for details).

Pitch 3A   5.7 ⚁

The third pitch of the West Buttress takes the prominent crack line skirting the left side of the bulging wall.

f. From the left end of the ledge head for a flared slot in a left-facing corner.

g. Though the moves in the corner are awkward, they are well-protected. This is a good place to practice your gyrating, stemming and chimneying skills. Easier climbing leads to a large, comfortable ledge about 70' up.

Pitch 3B   5.8+   ⚙

Another possibility is the fine third pitch of the West Face.

h. Climb the right side of the bulging wall to a natural chockstone, which, in true "old school" style, you can sling for protection. Better yet, plug in some large cams near the chockstone as well as up and right under the crux roof. Use long slings to avoid rope-drag.

i. The crux is quite "bouldery" and gymnastic on positive holds, and the climbing stays tricky until you're above the roof. As you study the sequence leading to the roof, bear in mind that you might smack the "rotten band" ledge if you peel.

Three moves above the roof you can plug in good gear and enjoy the situation . . .

j. The climbing above is pleasant, easy-to-protect 5.6. Finish on the large, comfortable ledge.

Pitch 4B   5.5   🦶

k. Pull over the bulge and trend up and right on big 'boilerplate' flakes to the summit.

Pitch 3C   5.5   ⚙

The third option, which offers the easiest line to the summit, has an interesting "mountaineering" feel to it. It follows the top of the West Chimney route, which is initially rather circuitous and marred by poor quality rock. Though the last part of the route also moves through bad rock, the climbing is easier.

l. From the block/ledge traverse right on the "rotten band." Although there is a paucity of protection, the climbing is easy. Don't overlook any possible placements. Use long slings to mitigate rope drag.

m. Getting established in the big dihedral involves sneaking past a pair of large, loose blocks sitting on a shelf (There's room to tiptoe around them!). Belay at the bottom of the large dihedral.

Pitch 4C   5.7   ♣

n. Your first challenge is the 15', low-angle "offwidth." Thankfully, a few face holds to the right spare you the horror of jamming this beast. The crack is about 6" wide and affords the only protection through this section.

o. Continue up the crack until you can make a balancey traverse right, thus avoiding a steep, awkward section in the crack above. The traverse is protected by an old pin halfway across.

p. Follow good cracks into the 10' wide chimney and belay within communicating distance of your partner. He'll appreciate the gesture, particularly on the balancey traverse.

Pitch 5C   5.4   🦶

q. The climbing from here to the walk-off ledge is easy.

Descent: For any of these finishes, follow the same descent as for Bastille Crack (see page 106).

Sandbagging

"Sandbagging" occupies a special niche in the climbing world. Sandbagging typically involves encouraging someone to try a route they'll most likely fail on, all the while withholding key beta (snicker, snicker). The amusement we get from watching our friends flail can be priceless, as long as nothing more than their pride is damaged.

Successful sandbagging relies on three elements: plausibility, creativity and a suitable victim. The first ascent of the Northcutt Start to the Bastille Crack in Eldorado Canyon is a classic tale of sandbagging. (See Bastille Crack section). Told that this tricky 5.10d start to the Bastille Crack had already been free-climbed by his rival Layton Kor (plausibility), Ray Northcutt (the suitable victim) was further suckered into bagging the line by the promise of good "hidden holds" (creativity). By firing the pitch and turning the sandbag on its end, Northcutt got the last laugh.

The third principle, that of finding a suitable victim, is generally a matter of opportunity. Sandbagging an overly-gullible climber is like shooting fish in a barrel—there's no sport in it. An ideal target would be someone who's just a little too full of themselves. The best defense, therefore, is to take your beta (whether solicited or not) with a grain of salt and a smidgen of modesty.

There are several variations on the sandbag, one being the "reverse sandbag." One day at Granite Mountain in Arizona, Rusty Baillie showed me and my partner a striking boulder problem he called "Death Mantle." He said it was deceptively hard . . . so hard in fact that it hadn't yet been done, even by local climbers we considered gods. He gave it a dramatic attempt, failed, then encouraged us to try it, saying he thought we were climbing pretty strong. I rose to the bait, launching myself at it like Achilles battering the walls of Troy, topping out after parlaying a heel-hook into a massive lurch for the lip. In triumph, I made a triumphant spectacle of myself, then turned around to see Rusty rolling on the ground, convulsed with laughter. Once the fit subsided, he grabbed his pack and sailed up "Death Mantle" which was, in fact, a lowly 5.6.

descent

Peanuts Wall
Star Wars

Lower Peanuts Wall

STAR WARS 5.8

This route is on Lower Peanuts Wall, an austere and isolated crag blessed with a relatively easy approach, shaded north-facing walls and inspiring views of the massive Redgarden Wall.

Pitch 1   5.7

a. Approach from the right (west) side of the crag along a prominent ledge system angling down and left.

b. The first pitch follows a wide corner with double cracks directly below the easily-identifiable hand crack on the second pitch.

c. The difficulties are modest and the protection is generous.

d. Belay on the ledge above.

e. On subsequent visits you may want to explore several other variations to the first pitch.

Pitch 2   5.8-

f. Negotiate a short band of suspect rock. Though you might dislodge something, it's easy to find a solid path through here. If even the smallest of rocks does fall, don't forget to shout "Rock!"

g. The 2" to 2.5" crack in the corner is the best hand-crack in Eldo. Before launching into it, visualize where you'll stop to place protection as well as the sizes you'll need (this parallel-sided fissure gobbles pieces in the 2" to 2 1/2" range). You're best off sinking cams from positions where you have a good foothold and a comfortable hand jam. The corner is steep and sustained—your ability to hang off a single jam while placing protection with the other hand will be put to the test. It's a good skill to learn.

h. Use smaller pieces for protection once you're in the flared slot. The angle eases off here and you can tuck your body into the flare to snag a quick rest.

i. Though the move over the little roof is awkward, you can place protection above your head.

j. Belay from a nice perch up top from which you can easily see your second.

Descent: Scramble further up the rock to a notch, from which you scramble down and west. Move slowly and carefully on this descent, as a fall here could be disastrous.

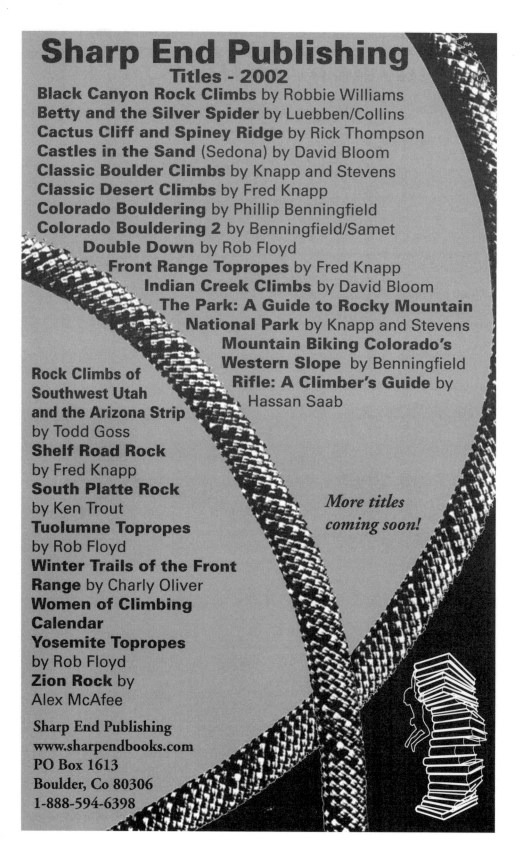

Sharp End Publishing
Titles - 2002

Black Canyon Rock Climbs by Robbie Williams

Betty and the Silver Spider by Luebben/Collins

Cactus Cliff and Spiney Ridge by Rick Thompson

Castles in the Sand (Sedona) by David Bloom

Classic Boulder Climbs by Knapp and Stevens

Classic Desert Climbs by Fred Knapp

Colorado Bouldering by Phillip Benningfield

Colorado Bouldering 2 by Benningfield/Samet

Double Down by Rob Floyd

Front Range Topropes by Fred Knapp

Indian Creek Climbs by David Bloom

The Park: A Guide to Rocky Mountain National Park by Knapp and Stevens

Mountain Biking Colorado's Western Slope by Benningfield

Rifle: A Climber's Guide by Hassan Saab

Rock Climbs of Southwest Utah and the Arizona Strip by Todd Goss

Shelf Road Rock by Fred Knapp

South Platte Rock by Ken Trout

Tuolumne Topropes by Rob Floyd

Winter Trails of the Front Range by Charly Oliver

Women of Climbing Calendar

Yosemite Topropes by Rob Floyd

Zion Rock by Alex McAfee

More titles coming soon!

Sharp End Publishing
www.sharpendbooks.com
PO Box 1613
Boulder, Co 80306
1-888-594-6398

Garden of the Gods

Climber on the Potholes Route, Red Spire
photo: Stewart M. Green

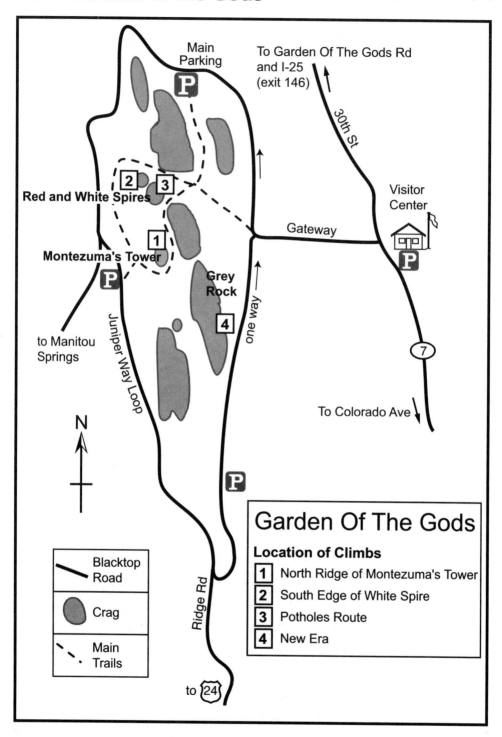

Main Parking

To Garden Of The Gods Rd and I-25 (exit 146)

30th St

Visitor Center

Red and White Spires

2 3

Gateway

Montezuma's Tower

1

Grey Rock

one way

to Manitou Springs

Juniper Way Loop

4

7

To Colorado Ave

N

Ridge Rd

Blacktop Road

Crag

Main Trails

Garden Of The Gods

Location of Climbs

1 North Ridge of Montezuma's Tower
2 South Edge of White Spire
3 Potholes Route
4 New Era

to 24

The Garden of the Gods

Climbers are attracted to this park by the inviting appearance of the steep fins, picturesque plates and the smooth rounded lamina. The Garden, with its backdrop of Pikes Peak, is an urban oasis of the desert Southwest. Red sandstone towers rise from tree-studded fields, offering climbers ample opportunity to bag summits. While the allure of towers attracts the vertically inclined, they soon find that the sandstone is actually not as hard as it looks and that the routes demand a disquieting and subtle sense of balance.

For the climber learning to lead in the traditional style, The Garden of the Gods can easily become an overwhelming experience. The rock is somewhat soft and strange, and the holds often sandy and sloping. Those who persevere in smearing up this learning curve will inevitably become accomplished face climbers.

The gamesmenship of English rock climbing was introduced here by Albert Ellingwood in 1914 and continued through Ormes and Boucher in the 20s, 30s and 40s. On the soft rock of the Garden you can literally and figuratively follow in the footsteps of some of Colorado's free climbing forefathers.

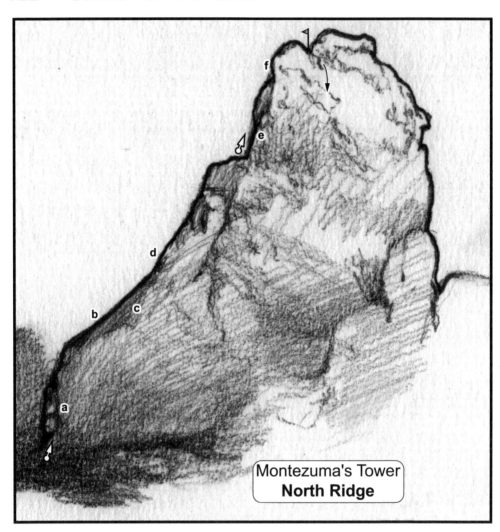

Montezuma's Tower
North Ridge

NORTH RIDGE OF MONTEZUMA'S TOWER 5.7

This summit is a worthy part of every climber's pilgrimage. It is a graceful part of the landscape and sees more ascents than any other technical climbing summit in the state. The crux occurs early, but as the walls on either side fall away and you tread lightly up the arete, you may be given occasion to pause. Good news: Stewart Green, a local climbing aficionado, says that he has never seen anyone actually fall from the North Ridge.

Pitch 1   5.7 R ⚙

a. At the north end of the tower you will find a large block. Look on the west side for a set of dimpled footholds made larger and more comfortable by years of use. A good medium-to-large stopper protects the moves up into these steps and a reach over the top of the block finds a comforting hold. Take care to treat this block gently.

b. The arete above is fairly runout up to the fixed pin, so place the best large nut that you can at your feet and trust your balance. Try to distribute your weight as evenly as possible on three of your limbs while moving the fourth. Remember that it is sometimes easier to lean and push on your palms downward than it is to try to pull upward with your arms outstretched above. Your hips should be directly above your weighted foot through the complete range of motion.

c. Above the fixed pin look to the right (west) side for a ledge with a natural thread hole on its opposite (south) end, and girth hitch it with a long enough sling (or slings) that you will not get ropedrag when you return to the arete.

d. Continue up the arete in the footsteps of all the previous pilgrims, past more fixed pins, and finally, to an easy crack. The belay is just above, on a ledge with fixed anchors and a nice view. You will be able to see and communicate more easily with your second if you sit nearer the top of the crack with an anchoring piece in the crack backed up by the fixed anchors.

Pitch 2   5.6 ⚙

e. Once again follow the worn steps to another crack where you may place protection for the moves up right. Bear in mind that cams exert considerable outward force; the sandstone flake forming the crack has its limitations. Don't take it for granite. You wouldn't likely generate a great deal of force if you fell before reaching the next fixed pin. Nevertheless, your belayer should be paying attention and not waving to the tourists.

f. The route should be easy to follow to the summit notch and the fixed anchor that awaits.

Descent: Rappel 140' to the ground. Two ropes are necessary.

White Twin Spire
South Edge

White Twin Spire

SOUTH EDGE 5.6

The route up the south ridge of this 60' fin gains a neat summit, and when you are done you can rappel or lower down the west face and set the rope up as a toprope for the various routes on that side.

a. Climb straight up the crack to a variety of protection possibilities.

b. Staying in the line of the discontinuous cracks allows you to supplement the two fixed pins, although the bold may find the moves to either side to be just as reasonable.

Descent: Rappel 60' down the west side to the ground.

Fred Knapp on the west face of White Spire
photo: Stewart M. Green

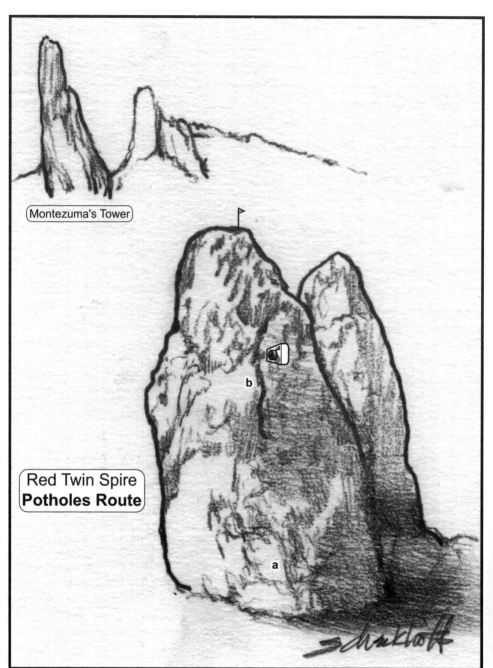

Montezuma's Tower

Red Twin Spire
Potholes Route

b

a

Red Twin Spire

POTHOLES ROUTE 5.7

It will probably become evident that the redder rock is softer than the whiter rock. It may be better to get comfortable on the compact, gritty white rock first. The classic Potholes Route is the easiest path to the summit of this 70' fin.

a. Begin at a series of flake holds on the northeast corner and find some surprisingly good gear placements and incut holds as you move towards the first of four fixed pins.

b. Weave through "The Potholes" on your way to the summit. If you set up a toprope you can experiment with impunity on this soft rock.

Descent: Rappel 70' to the ground.

Grey Rock - **New Era**

Grey Rock

The gray rock in the park is more solid than the red and this formation (which is sometimes known by other names) offers a fine collection of routes. The rock is more textured and sometimes beautifully featured.

NEW ERA 5.7

This route is easy to find—look for the prominent dihedral not far to the left of a prominent chimney. Most climbers know something of Harvey Carter's career as a climber—he did first ascents of many classics—but did you know he had a professional baseball career as well? He could throw a 102 mph fastball. That, and an ERA (earned run average) of 5.70 would be good enough for a job with the Rockies.

Pitch 1 5.7 ❖

a. Work out a plan for getting going in the thin crack; either from the left or the right.

b. After loading the crack with excellent protection, face climb over the bulge (5.7).

c. Easier climbing takes you to a fixed anchor. One rope is sufficient for a rappel from here.

Pitch 2 5.7 ❖

d. It is easier to climb out on the left wall rather than try the squeeze-play in the crack.

e. At a point about 12' below the belay niche you are, more or less, forced to keep your hands in the crack but you have a choice with your feet—either stem them out or walk them up the rock and layback. Stemming, though requiring more flexibility, balance and subtlety, is less strenuous than laybacking. Whatever you do, the protection is excellent.

f. Rappelling (two ropes) is possible from the fixed anchor here. If time is running short, this rappel may be a good idea as the final pitch is pretty runout and the descent takes time.

Pitch 3 5.4 ❀

g. The easiest of several options is to step right from the niche and climb to a comfortable spot (5.4).

h. Work left and up (large slings are helpful but not critical).

i. Many sequences are possible. Think of this as a 5.3 boulder problem, one where you can stand comfortably nearly everywhere. There is a fixed pin up and left but the climbing is somewhat easier up and right.

j. Follow the arete to the scenic summit.

Descent: Be aware that this "walk-off" descent involves a fair amount of downclimbing. There are no fixed rappel anchors on the upper section of this descent and arranging your own anchors in the event of darkness or an emergency would be quite difficult. Begin by descending a pair of chimney/ gullies to the south and arrive at a slab. Friction down to the east. Some bolt anchors are visible near the bottom, but reaching them is quite dangerous; it is best to continue the scramble. I recommend scoping out this descent route from the ground before you begin, particularly if time will be a factor.

Fixed Protection

Whilst climbing a route (including routes described in this book) you may come across fixed protection. Though its presence can be reassuring, bear in mind that not all fixed protection is created equal. The fixed piton may have been left on purpose or by mistake; in either case, fixed pins should be treated with suspicion. The strength of fixed pins can rarely be evaluated by sight alone—they may be older or weaker than they appear. Always back up fixed pins with gear of your own.

Bolts come in all shapes and sizes, making them just as difficult to evaluate as fixed pins. Old 1/4" bolts are not to be trusted at all. Even a 3/8" bolt used to hold no more than body weight will develop "metal fatigue" over time, shortening its life span to as little as 15 years. **Never rely on one piece of gear** (even a bolt) to anchor a toprope, belay or rappel.

Fixed pieces are convenient, particularly at belay anchors and on rappel routes. However, gear you place yourself is gear you know the strength of; use it whenever possible!

In the Front Range the practice of deliberately fixing protection on routes was developed by Harvey Carter at the Garden of the Gods near Colorado Springs. The placing of fixed pins protected the soft sandstone of the Garden from scarring by the repeated pounding and extraction of pins.

As climbing gear became more sophisticated it became possible to set good protection in cracks without scarring them permanently. Chocks, nuts and eventually Friends could be removed just as easily as they were placed, leaving the rock intact. This development, coupled with the talents of gifted climbers like Henry Barber and Jim Erickson, advanced the concept of "calculated risk" on rock, pushing standards and ushering in the "Golden Age" of free climbing. Pioneers from this era left behind routes which still embody the spirit of our sport.

Today's concern about the establishment of fixed protection reflects a variety of interests. The traditional ethic tolerates a bare minimum of fixed protection, holding that this approach best preserves the essential climbing experience. "Sport climbers," who favor an abundance of fixed pieces, feel that removing "risk" from the "calculation" is both convenient and fun. While placing fixed protection near good natural placements is not justifiable, the security offered by a series of fat, shiny bolts does allow for a more relaxed approach to rock climbing. It's a style not unlike figure skating, where hard moves and gymnastic sequences can be rehearsed in relative safety.

Climbers on Crack Parallel (5.7), The Pinnacle. photo: Stewart M. Green

North Cheyenne Canyon

North Cheyenne Canyon is home to a creek which plunges over Helen Hunt Falls and cascades past granite slabs and towers, charming the rock into phantasmagoric shapes. Climbers from the US Army, who left their marks anonymously up and down the Front Range, pioneered a three-pitch route on a large tower, and decades later the "Army Route" on The Pinnacle gives climbers the "urban-alpine" experience of being on a miniature mountain.

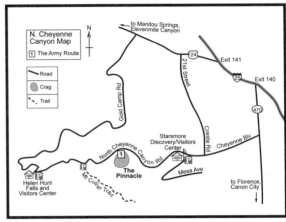

Cheyenne Canyon
The Pinnacle

The Pinnacle

ARMY ROUTE 5.5

Pitch 1   5.5

a. The best way to gain entrance to the large obtuse dihedral is by traversing along a crack from the right. This method also affords the most protection. The first moves into the corner can be protected with a medium-sized stopper.

b. The rock here is amazingly solid and offers pleasurable climbing with many opportunities for good natural protection. You will notice on this pitch that many huge bolts have been cut off. With clean gear this good, why drill holes?

c. Pass a small roof on the left and follow the corner system to a belay ledge on the left. A large bolt is found here.

If you wish to do only this pitch and avoid the gravelly sections on the upper pitches (and miss the view from the summit) then you can rappel with two ropes (or possibly one sixty-meter rope) from a pair of huge bolts on the slab to your left (east). Remain tied in for the traverse and downclimb to these anchors; have the first climber place protection for the last and strongest climber.

Pitch 2   5.5

d. Step left a little and then follow a series of large bolts up until, just when you think the angle is becoming pedestrian, you follow a ledge/crack to the right. This avoids the crumbly rock of the left-facing corner and takes you out to better rock on the face.

e. After passing another huge bolt you will have to rely a little on the "leader must not fall" principle as you weave up and then left to follow the path of least resistance leading to the belay ledge above. The steps you take will be gravelly and about 5.4 or easier if you avoid excessive gyrations and seek out the simplest moves.

f. In the center of the face is a crack that takes a large cam. It is also possible to diagonal past this to reach the belay ledge from the right side.

Pitch 3   5.5

g. Another large bolt protects the climbing over slightly steeper steps of granular rock. This provides an exercise in balance, as too much lurching around seems to disturb the piles. Keep your weight over your feet.

h. The next bolt protects the moves up to and over the next gibbosity, after which the summit appears. A belay anchor, on the stance near the summit, is found at foot level.

Descent: Downclimb carefully to the south and down the gravel slopes to the col. From there a trail slides you down to the west and terra firma.

Bouldering

Climbing without a rope is the purest form of climbing. Although the maxim "the leader must not fall" has been modified over time, there are still cases when it rings true. It's times like these when the lessons you learn bouldering will come in handy.

Bouldering encourages you become adept at moving over rock by helping you develop a larger repertoire of movements and techniques. On different types and angles of rock you can learn: crimp, pinch and open-handed grips, finger locks and jams of all sizes, and edging and smearing techniques for your feet. The key is incorporating all these techniques into a series of fluid movements.

From the first time you touch rock you'll learn that balance and body position are crucial to your ability to move. On low-angle rock you'll learn how to shift your weight while palming and smearing. On steep and overhanging rock you can back-step and twist to extend your reach. However, these are but a handful of techniques. The more you climb, the more you'll learn about moving efficiently. And the more organic your repertoire becomes to your climbing technique, the more pleasure you will get from each climb. Even mantling can be fun if you take the time to master it!

Resting techniques are a crucial part of your repertoire. Chimneying and stemming positions allow you to rest your upper body. Elbow-locks and knee-bars are effective rests, even on overhanging stone. Sometimes just palming against a corner with your arms lower than your heart will help your poor, pumped forearms recover. Standing on your outside edge, instead of the ball of your foot, will help you de-pump your tired achy calves. You'll often find yourself resting one part of your body while another part works to keep you attached!

I cannot overemphasize the importance of down-climbing. It's valuable both because it extends your comfort zone beyond a rest (because you can return to the rest after exploring the situation above) and because it allows you to back down in case of trouble or poor route-finding. As with all climbing skills, the more you practice, the more natural it will feel.

Down-climbing feels quite awkward initially because you can't see your feet, forcing you to "fish" for footholds. This shortcoming is compensated for by the fact that you don't have to fight gravity, using it instead to help you "sag" down onto holds. While bouldering, practice down-climbing until you become more comfortable with it. Next time you're on the sharp end you'll find that down-climbing to a rest is often preferable to hanging on until the bitter end.

Another bouldering skill that translates to lead climbing is the ability to jump off in control. In situations where a fall seems both "safe" and inevitable, it's preferable to drop in control than to go cart-wheeling over like a lawn chair blown by a gust of wind. One disadvantage to developing a talent and penchant for jumping off is that it may become preferable to actually trying.

South Platte Area

Climbers on Left Handed Jew, Turkey Perch   photo: Stewart M. Green

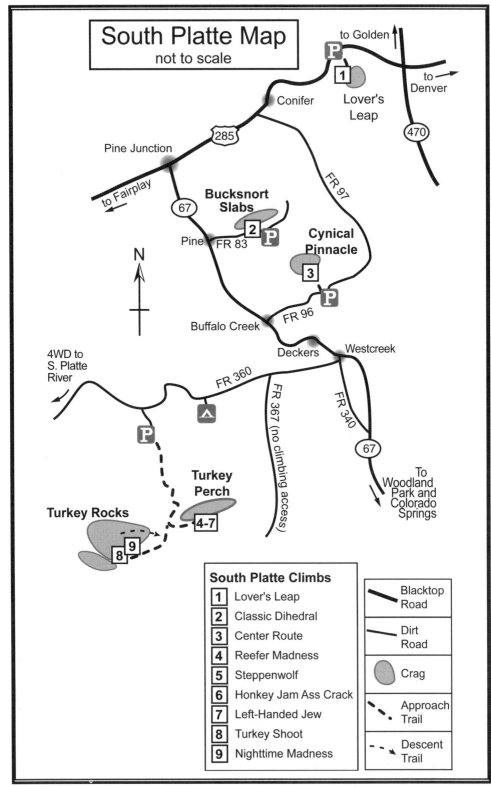

South Platte Map
not to scale

to Golden

P

1

to Denver

Conifer

Lover's Leap

285

470

Pine Junction

to Fairplay

FR 97

67

Bucksnort Slabs

2

P

Pine   FR 83

Cynical Pinnacle

3

P

N

Buffalo Creek

FR 96

Deckers   Westcreek

4WD to S. Platte River

FR 360

FR 367 (no climbing access)

FR 340

67

To Woodland Park and Colorado Springs

P

Turkey Perch

4-7

Turkey Rocks

8 9

South Platte Climbs		Blacktop Road
1	Lover's Leap	Dirt Road
2	Classic Dihedral	Crag
3	Center Route	
4	Reefer Madness	Approach Trail
5	Steppenwolf	
6	Honkey Jam Ass Crack	Descent Trail
7	Left-Handed Jew	
8	Turkey Shoot	
9	Nighttime Madness	

South Platte

The South Platte drainage is a vast region of over a thousand square miles. Visitors immediately notice the overwhelming presence of granite domes and blocks throughout its high forests. Despite the abundance of rock, much of the Platte remains unclimbed. The best routes are found on the south faces; thus clear winter days can be warm. Yet, surprisingly, the Platte's elevation can provide an escape from summer's heat.

On the archetypal Platte route you will find subtle face climbing and pure crack climbing. The former can be minimally protected while the latter can eat gear by the armful. The routes I have chosen should prepare you for quintessential granite climbs in such premier venues as Yosemite or Joshua Tree.

Routes that are too isolated are not included in this reference due to the wilderness nature of the outlying crags. Snakes, mountain lions, lightning and isolation provide experiences worth savoring only after whetting your palate on the domesticated roadside rock. Having said that, I would suggest that a day at Cynical Pinnacle will appeal more to your feral nature.

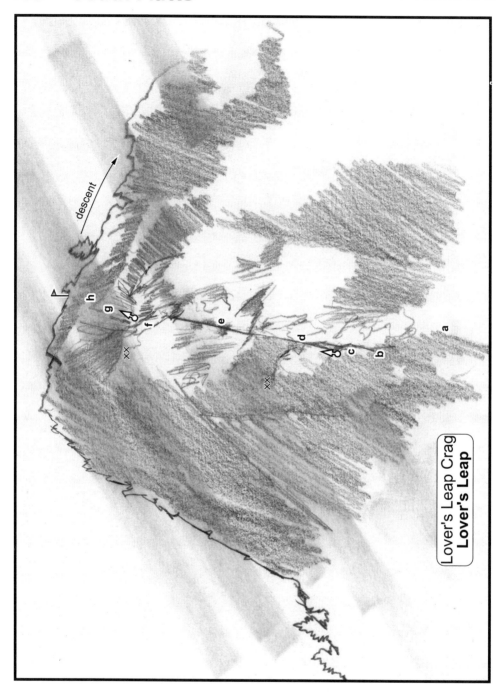

Lover's Leap Crag
Lover's Leap

Lover's Leap

Although the name may beckon the heartbroken, this crag is actually more solid than it appears. It sits in the eastern cleft of foothills through which both Hwy 285 and Turkey Creek run, and while the sound of traffic never seems to completely disappear, the road provides easy access. This is one of the few north-facing (read: summer) crags in the book. The directissima is also called Lover's Leap and is of the most interest to the beginning leader.

Approach the cliff by crossing the creek where possible and bushwhacking east of the drainage/talus.

LOVER'S LEAP 5.7+ 🧗 🧗 🧗 🧗

Pitch 1   5.6 ❖

a. Begin near the lowest point of rock, left of a large, broken-up, riparian recess (where you first reach the wall after approaching up the talus). Navigate a series of low-angle, blocky ledges (5.4) to gain a major left-facing corner system that spans the wall, albeit disjointedly, from bottom to top. Another convenient landmark is the patch of bright-green lichen just right of the corner itself.

b. Climb out right of a short corner a little way up the main corner. Take care with the two wedged blocks, which seem secure enough if you don't pull on them.

c. Solve a little "slot traverse" problem to arrive at a good belay ledge. A large block roughly the shape and size of a coffin is perched on this ledge!

Pitch 2   5.6 ❖

d. Tackle a series of short 5.5 and 5.6 sections with rests between them. Soon after passing the "coffin," scope left along a ledge for a 3-bolt anchor (useful if you need to escape via rappel). A double-rope rappel from a station near the top of this pitch will get you back to these bolts.

e. Climb the short prominent crack, which is wide enough to be seen from the road.

f. Either belay where the corner fades into a blocky ledge system or continue up and left through a stepped section to a belay ledge at the bottom of a square recess containing steeper cracks.

Pitch 3   5.7+ ❖

g. The more obvious crack above is quite good and quite "interesting." (Note: in trad-climbing jargon, "interesting" is usually a synonym for difficult). Several key holds keep the crack in the 5.7 range; the climbing is just balancey enough to be "interesting."

h. Set an anchor at the top of this pitch by backing up the old bolt with a good fixed pin. Better yet, back up both of these relics with gear of your own!

Descent: Walk off to the southwest then around to the north. Given the 3-bolt anchor on the ledge near the start of the last pitch, it's surprising that there isn't a set on top as well, providing a rap route down the entire crag. Were there one, lovers need not have leapt!

Bucksnort Slabs
Classic Dihedral

Bucksnort Slabs

This little roadside crag near the town of Pine is only one-fifth of a mile from the infamous Bucksnort Saloon. Another nearby attraction is "Reggie's Will-o-the-Wisp" restaurant, a mile or so south of Pine Junction on Hwy 285. Reggie has a jazz trio, which plays three or four nights a week. Across the road from the slabs is a cascading creek featuring a water-sculpted stream cavern . . . totally tubular and way cool!

The Bucksnort Slabs are on private property. The landowners permit climbing activity as long as the area is kept clean and climbers don't intrude on them. Please respect their wishes.

CLASSIC DIHEDRAL 5.7

This is also known, cryptically, as "The Crack of Anticipation." You will learn to climb polished rock.

Pitch 1 5.7 ⅄

a. Situated smack dab in the middle of the crag, this dihedral more resembles an open book than a corner. At the bottom of the dihedral find a large squarish block with a pretty crack starting halfway up it. Climbing this crack rather than the side of the block is roughly 5.4.

b. You may want to belay from the ledge at the base of the crack to escape the dirt.

c. You'll encounter several sections of 5.7, the first of which comes on fast. The excellent protection should inspire confidence, so practice standing on your feet as much as possible.

d. The moves linking the good finger crack with a wider, hand-sized section pose another 5.7 crux. Again, good footwork is of the essence.

e. As the crack widens it forces you to alter your tactics. You'll probably find that it's easier to lean off the crack and work your feet than rely on jamming alone. Experiment with different techniques . . . your gear is good and the rock kicks back at a comfortable angle.

f. Clip into the slings around the natural chockstone, preferably with another long sling. You'll appreciate the pro on the 5.7 layback moves above.

g. A 150' rappel from a bolt anchor out left gets you back down. Though perfect style should involve following a route to the top, I can't especially recommend it in this case. The summit is pointless, the second pitch lacks the aesthetics of the first one, and the leader could rap down and clean the gear so the whole party can take turns leading this great pitch. Cleaning your own gear is a great way to get a feel for how good your placements are.

Pitch 2 5.7 ✤

h. Luckily, an alternative passage up and left of the belay exists to this unprotected 5.5 slab.

i. The regular second pitch continues up the original crack past another section of 5.7.

j. Angle right and follow a groove to the top, amidst the large blocks.

Descent: If you decide to do the second pitch, walk off to the south (left), a pleasant though gravelly stroll through the pines.

h

g

f

e

d

xxxx

c

b

a start in gully
(hidden behind
buttress)

approach

Cynical Pinnacle - **Center Route**

Cynical Pinnacle

This beautiful granite spire ought to provide inspiration for even the most jaded Front Range misanthrope. It has eye-catching pure lines, one of the most prominent of which is Center Route, predictably located in the center of the south face. It is paralleled by the spectacular Wunsch's Dihedral just to the left.

CENTER ROUTE   5.9+

Approach: Park in a small pullout just east of the much larger Dome parking area. The trail is breathtakingly direct. Swerve right and aim for a gully at the foot of the spire. Scramble up this gully with some awkward steps. The start is pretty obvious up and just right at the top of the gully. The approach is by far the longest and steepest of any in this book, so pack a headlamp or flashlight just in case.

Pitch 1   5.8 ⚒

a. Well.... I may be lying. Remember how I told you to take all advice with a grain of salt? This first 10' section might have a move of 5.9 in it. Get up to the ledge and walk right to join the beautiful hand and finger crack.

b. Stoppers and hexes can sometimes work even better than cams in some of these placements.

c. Belay in a niche. Take care with your rope not to let strands fall down into the cracks below as this can lead to them getting stuck! Piling the rope on the stance will often work but can get in the way. Best is to loop it back and forth over your knee as you take it in, then replace your knee with a sling to hang it out of the way. The loops will feed out as you pay out the rope on the next pitch. Try making the first loop quite long, then each successive loop a little shorter, so they don't get tangled.

Pitch 2   5.9+ ♣

d. This pitch offers good protection and generally good jams, but the lack of real rests make your endurance the issue. In your favor is the fact that it is usually less than vertical. It is critical to climb efficiently. Use your feet well. Target the next hand jam (never more than two moves away) and move to it smoothly. Wired stoppers work well in this pitch and each hand jam offers the opportunity to place another one. But remember—the longer you hang out placing stoppers, the more you test your endurance—a classic dilemma.

When hand jamming up a sustained crack (or just jamming too tight on an easier one), it is your thumbs which will give out. Remember, "opposable thumbs" separate us from the apes, so don't squander them!

To add to the drama, when the thumbs go you'll find yourself struggling just to clip and unclip carabiners, let alone pulling back the triggers on your cams . . . Good luck.

e. Belay in the cozy niche. This is great for married couples, but if you like to be able to breathe you might consider using the stance above the niche also. One person in each. Be careful with the wedged block, it shifts alarmingly if you stand on the back of it.

Pitch 3   5.8+ ⚸

f. The chimney above may look intimidating, but there is a great 2" to 2.5" crack on the left wall.

g. Face holds keep appearing to take the strain off the arms.

h. The route ends on this shoulder. If you want to go to the top of the spire you need to climb the suave Class Act (5.11b) above you.

Descent: Two different rappel descents can be used here: one down the backside (down Rap Crack), and one down the front-side. Both require two ropes.

If you go down the backside, scramble down the gully to the east. This gully has a couple awkward steps past large boulders. Look out for poison ivy lower down. Keep to the right as you get below the boulders and try to locate a 3-foot high tunnel in a horizontal break near the bottom of the gully that takes you to the front-side! (This saves an exposed and much longer traverse around the corner).

If you go down the more popular front-side rappel, hold the ropes when you get to the bolt anchor on the face. If a breeze blows the rope-ends out of reach they may never come back and you will be stuck with no way down. Throwing the rope may send it into the wider cracks and get it stuck. You may want to lower the ends of the rope and tie on some weight (a water bottle or some large hexes for example) to keep them from drifting away (these will also act as "stopper knots" in the ends!) If the wind is reaching "Perfect Storm" velocities, it is best to lower the first person.

John Christie demonstrates fine jamming technique on pitch three of Center Route.

Etiquette

Believe it or not, **you** are not the only climber in the Front Range. You share the cliffs with (many) others, and mutual respect starts with **you**. Here are several issues that always come up:

Leave no trace. This applies to everything from tape and beer cans to human waste. You know the routine. Pack out the former and bury the latter well away from the crag. As with everything else in this book, the key is to anticipate.

Don't alter the climbs. Other than removing dangerously loose rock, you shouldn't change what you find in place at the cliff. Learn to work with what's there instead of making the rock conform to your needs! Don't plow new trails—you're better off walking on established trails or exposed rock.

Your dog may be *your* best friend, but to others he may be threatening or just plain annoying. Don't tell people that "he won't bite." Many people have been bitten by dogs that "don't bite." Unfortunately, dogs tend to run over other people's belongings and tear up the off-trail environment. Barking and canine antics can also be very distracting to other climbers, whose attention should be focused on their climbing and belaying. If you must bring your dog to the crag, please keep him on a leash. If he starts to bark, please take him home.

Children pose many of the same problems that dogs do. If children are appropriately well-mannered then going to the crag can be a valuable experience for them. But as a parent your attention will always be divided, a situation with potentially dire consequences.

Avoid unnecessary chatter when others are climbing within earshot. Leading and belaying require concentration—you may be detracting from the focus and pleasure of your peers' climbing experience.

A common theme throughout this book is "awareness and anticipation." This applies to social interaction as well. In general, our shared love for climbing allows us to enjoy each other's company.

descent

d
c
b
a

Turkey Perch - **Reefer Madness**

Turkey Rocks

Front Range climbers have made pilgrimages to Turkey Rocks since the 1960s. This cluster of excellent granite crags features a concentration of crack climbing unparalleled in the rest of the state. The best climbers in Colorado's history have practiced their art here. The 8000' elevation adds coolness by degrees in the summer and the south faces can be warm in winter months. Nearby camping makes this a great weekend destination.

As an aspiring leader, you may first be attracted to Turkey Perch due to the comparatively short length of its routes. Take heart—after a few routes here, the more impressive Turkey Rock will seem approachable. This 350' crag requires more involved route-finding and a higher level of commitment on its multi-pitch routes. Retreating from Turkey Rock usually entails leaving your own gear behind for anchors. Gear is replaceable; you aren't. Don't be shy about bailing if you see a gnarly thunderstorm rolling in. Lightning is a serious concern at Turkey Rocks—the routes finish on the summit and lightning loves to travel down crack systems. As for the climbing difficulties, remember that as the Chinese book I Ching advises: "perseverance furthers."

Approach: From Westcreek proper (about a half mile from the turn-off), continue 0.8 miles south on County Road 68 (gravel). Turn west on Stump Road (Road 68) and travel about 2.5 miles to Forest Road 360. Follow this another 1.7 miles to Big Turkey Campground. Most parties continue on rougher terrain for another 0.8 miles to the unmarked Turkey Rock turn-off on the left. Follow a rough road to a parking area. A trail switchbacks to a saddle. Head left for Turkey Perch and head right to reach Turkey Rock.

Turkey Perch

The Perch hosts a great collection of one-pitch routes. Though a popular toprope venue (bring ultra-long slings for the anchors), the Perch is also an excellent place to hone your leading skills. If you successfully toprope a route, give serious consideration to leading it. While toproping, search for the best gear placements and positions from which to place pro. Time invested in honing your leading skills on routes like these will pay dividends on multi-pitch routes.

Reefer Madness 5.8

Nearly every move is kind, bud.

a. The initial right-facing corner is technical enough to be the crux. It's thin.

b. The good hand crack leads to a leaning crack that poses subtle balance problems. If you can't peer into the crack it will be hard to place gear . . . plan ahead.

c. For most leaders on this pitch, the psychological crux comes when the crack ends at the slab. Place a good piece before you stand up and trust your feet on the face holds.

d. Exit to the left.

Turkey Perch - **Steppenwolf**

STEPPENWOLF 5.9 ✤

a. The initial offwidth can be overcome using the hidden crack inside, allowing you to avoid the usual embarrassing grovelling. It's the "hidden holds trick."

b. The crack above requires good footwork and sequential thinking.

c. The technical crux comes when the crack narrows to a less secure size. Place good gear for the little runout above.

d. The face climbing is exciting but brief, with good holds.

e. The finishing crack is straightforward and triumphant.

HONKEY JAM ASS CRACK 5.7 ✤

What a charming and eloquent name that has been bestowed on this otherwise excellent route!

a. There are two options at the start, the left one being easier.

b. The right-hand start is more problematic. I suggest clipping into a good piece in the crack out right (Left-Handed Jew) with a long sling to back up the small nut in the corner.

c. Once in the main crack you will find little to impede your progress.

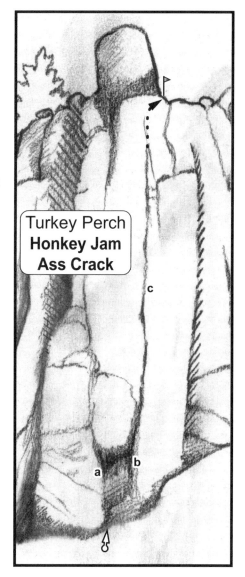

Turkey Perch
**Honkey Jam
Ass Crack**

Turkey Perch
Left-Handed Jew

Left-Handed Jew 5.7 ❧

a. Even though you may be initially put off by its size, this crack offers pure, straightforward fun.

b. Place good gear to protect the traverse. A long sling helps the rope run smoothly and won't lengthen any potential falls. The belayer should keep a little slack in the system to avoid swinging the leader back into the corner.

c. The traverse is most easily done low. Though there isn't much for the hands, you'll be strolling across on good footholds. On traverses like this, with poor handholds, it is usually best to keep you feet fairly close to each other. The smaller the steps you take, the easier it is to feel balanced.

d. Step up into the crack that starts at the rooflet. Take advantage of the comfortable stance here to place pro and . . . relax. After you step up into and through the bulge, the rest of the pitch will pass easily.

descent

i

h
g

f

e

d

c

b

a

Turkey Rock - **Turkey Shoot**

TURKEY SHOOT 5.9

This route takes its name from the fact that the first ascent party was shot at by irate local homeowners. Hopefully your motivation to finish the climb will come from within. Take multiples of protection for hand-sized cracks and a couple of 5"-6" pieces.

Pitch 1   5.7

a. Begin in a pair of wide cracks. Though protection might be problematic, you can milk the well-placed face holds and stem to avoid most of the wide-crack terrors. Start in the right-hand crack before switching over to the left one.

b. The transition into the left crack is made more secure by an elbow lock.

c. The best belay is at the large chockstone.

Pitch 2   5.9-

d. The difficulties start immediately. Scum your way into a full-body jam in the wide crack to reach a hand jam that allows access to the beautiful hand crack above.

e. As you place gear here consider the possibility of rope drag after the traverse into the crack out right. Good footholds keep the traverse moderate (5.7), much like the crack above.

f. Belay at this blocky stance. If you're not plagued by rope-drag and/or altitude sickness then continue to the larger ledge above.

Pitch 3   5.8

g. The offwidth crack in the corner is short so you can get by with two 5"-6" pieces. Despite its size, most people won't experience the dreaded "offwidth" anguish. Start by facing right and chimney between the left wall and a feature on the right wall.

h. Having chimneyed as high as you can, it's now time to turn around. Face holds on the left wall help you through the last bit of this section.

i. Follow the crack to the top, encountering a few moderately difficult but brief sections along the way.

Descent: Descend from the top of Turkey Rock via a walk-off/scramble to the east. Stay near the south face as you approach the eastern end and weave through the large boulders.

descent

Turkey Rock
**Nighttime
Madness**

NIGHTTIME MADNESS 5.7/5.8

This climb has a little of everything—the pitches are short with many possible variations. For those hungering for the experience of a multi-pitch route, Nighttime Madness offers a nibble off everything at the buffet table!

Pitch 1 5.7

a. Start near a large tree and head up the well-featured crack. Good hand jams take you through the crux.

b. If you're so inclined, you can follow the 5.7 continuation which starts from a stance on the left.

c. Directly above the first section the crack gets a little harder (maybe 5.8) with good jams.

d. Belay on the ledge. This ledge leads right across the wall to a double-bolt anchor, making for an easy escape.

Pitch 2 5.7

e. Two possibilities, neither harder than 5.7, take you to another ledge. You have two options above here.

f. The "bomb-bay" crack on the left goes at roughly 5.8. Climbing a chimney like this in shorts and a tee-shirt provides a lesson in both technique and suffering, reinforcing the Nietzschean maxim that "That which fails to kill me only makes me stronger." Notice escape sling.

g. The crack in the corner out right (5.7) presents a more graceful option.

h. Belay on the ledge above.

Pitch 3 5.7 or 5.8

i. On the left end of the ledge is the last pitch of Turkey Shoot, a moderate (5.8) offwidth requiring no real offwidth technique.

j. Nighttime Madness continues up a faint corner above that swerves right.

k. Either continue up the original Madness line (5.6) or enter the dark embrace of the neighboring chimney via a short traverse right.

l. The chimney is actually pretty cool! By face-climbing on the left, employing the odd wedging maneuver and making crab-like forays to the back of the chimney for gear, you can tame this beast at a mere 5.8.

Descent: Descend from the top of Turkey Rock via a walk-off/scramble to the east. Stay near the south face as you approach the eastern end and weave through the large boulders.

Aid Climbing

Aid climbing, as a means to an end, has always been a part of climbing. It has value for the free-climber as a method of learning about and testing gear placements. Hanging from a piece of gear you've placed yourself has a marvelous way of focusing your attention. You'll quickly find out just what the piece is capable of—and sometimes what it's not!

Beginning leaders should make a point of climbing a few clean aid pitches in order to become proficient at both placing gear and assessing its holding power. You don't have to lead them all, but do lead *at least* one. If your goal is to become adept at placing gear on free climbs then it's better to experiment with a variety of different-sized placements. If you're training to do a big-wall route then you'll need to practice your speed and high-stepping technique. This book mentions a few good routes for practicing clean aid, of which there are many in the Front Range.

Elevenmile Canyon

Turret Dome

photo: Stewart M. Green

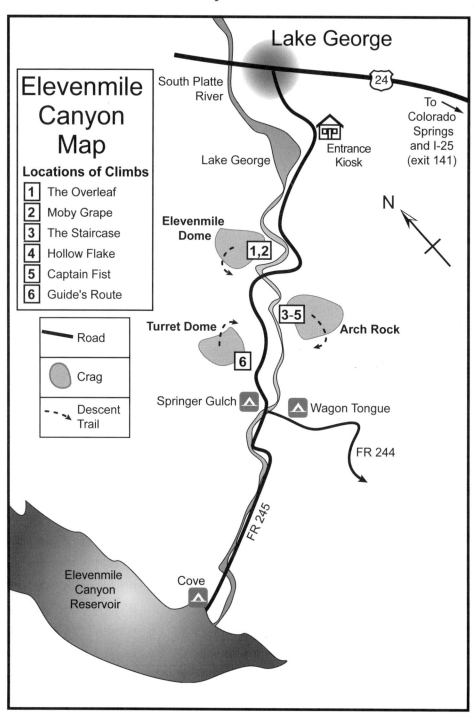

Lake George

Elevenmile Canyon Map

Locations of Climbs

1 The Overleaf
2 Moby Grape
3 The Staircase
4 Hollow Flake
5 Captain Fist
6 Guide's Route

—— Road

Crag

- - - → Descent Trail

South Platte River

Lake George

24

To Colorado Springs and I-25 (exit 141)

Entrance Kiosk

N

Elevenmile Dome

1,2

3-5

Turret Dome

Arch Rock

6

Springer Gulch

Wagon Tongue

FR 244

FR 245

Elevenmile Canyon Reservoir

Cove

Elevenmile Canyon

With the South Platte River winding through it and a multitude of alluring crags above, this picturesque canyon is an idyllic place to both camp and climb. The canyon generally runs north-south, offering plenty of easily-accessed climbs in the sun or shade.

The few routes described below should whet your appetite. There are hundreds of routes here and plenty of potential for exploration and discovery. You can learn everything you need to know about trad climbing in this canyon.

To reach Elevenmile Canyon, take I-25 to the US 24 exit in Colorado Springs. Follow Highway 24 through Woodland Park (a little confusing—stay left) to the town of Lake George. Take a left at Park County Road 96 and follow this for about a mile to the Elevenmile Canyon Park entrance station. Pay the fee and enter the canyon. Elevenmile Dome is located about 2.75 miles from the station. Arch Rock is about 4 miles and Turret Dome is about 4.25.

Elevenmile Dome
The Overleaf

Elevenmile Dome

This crag offers excellent face climbing pitches with various degrees of protection. Park near The Overleaf towards the west end of the dome. Check out these two naturally-protected lines:

THE OVERLEAF 5.8+

Pitch 1 5.8+ ❖

a. Work up the slab into the long, right-facing corner system. Step up to place protection in the crack on the short rightward traverse (5.5), then climb the face down and right before returning to the crack for a slightly steeper section.

b. Similarly, as you approach the crux roof continue to place protection in the crack but face climb out right. Hopefully you've rationed your larger pieces on the lower section, as you'll want them at the crux.

c. The problematic crux comes on steeply and suddenly! Good protection and perfect hand jams lead to the roof. Move back left a couple of moves until you're squatting on one bulge and tucked beneath another (Shorter people will be at an advantage here!). Lean out on great jams to place protection above the overhang, taking care not to plug up any crucial holds. You can easily return to the "resting" squat and repeat the move out to the lip of the roof until you're satisfied with the arrangement of your pro. Though your feet might cut loose on the crux, remember that you're plugged into hand jams a dozen fishermen couldn't pull you out of. The crux involves getting your foot up on something . . . something like that edge out left!

d. An optional belay here could help communication with your second (this means that you'll need to do a short additional pitch to reach a better belay up high).

Note: If you keep the rope too tight on your second while he's following a roof you'll pull him off. Keep too much slack in the line and, if he falls, he'll end up dangling in space, unable to reach the rock. At this point you can either lower him or have him prussic back up. Good communication is crucial in this type of situation!

e. Alternately, skirt the crux roof by following a large flake out right, necessitating a runout to regain the main crack.

Pitch 2 5.6 ⚐

f. If you belayed right above the roof you'll need to do the aforementioned 30' pitch to this higher belay, from which you can reach the top of the crack in a single push. Belay on the big ledge under the caprock.

Descent: Follow the walk-off ledge to the left, until it is obvious to head down.

Elevenmile Dome
Moby Grape

Moby Grape 5.7

Pitch 1   5.7

a. Climb up into the obvious right-facing dihedral and follow a thin crack with good finger locks and small gear placements.

b. Though the left wall offers good holds, be aware of a few loose blocks perched there as well.

c. If you haven't brought a surplus of small stoppers and cams, you'll need to ration your gear. Save a couple of 1.5" size pieces for the end of the pitch; use the rest of your larger pieces whenever possible to save the small stuff.

d. The bulge at the end of the pitch takes good "thin-hands" sized gear.

e. One 60-meter rope (or two shorter ropes) gets you down from the double-bolt anchor.

Pitch 2   5.6-

f. Traverse left about 20' and belay. Though short, this diminutive pitch makes for easier communication and fewer rope-drag hassles on the next pitch.

Pitch 3   5.5

g. Angle up and left. Short technical problems (a move or two) interrupt easier sections of climbing. With many variations possible and few landmarks to go on, your route-finding skills will be pressed into service. Plan ahead lest you paint yourself into the proverbial corner!

h. The rock is generally quite good though a few things might pull off. There could be people below so climb carefully. Belay on or near the large ledge below the steep "cap."

Descent: Walk left on the ledge to a point from which you can easily downclimb.

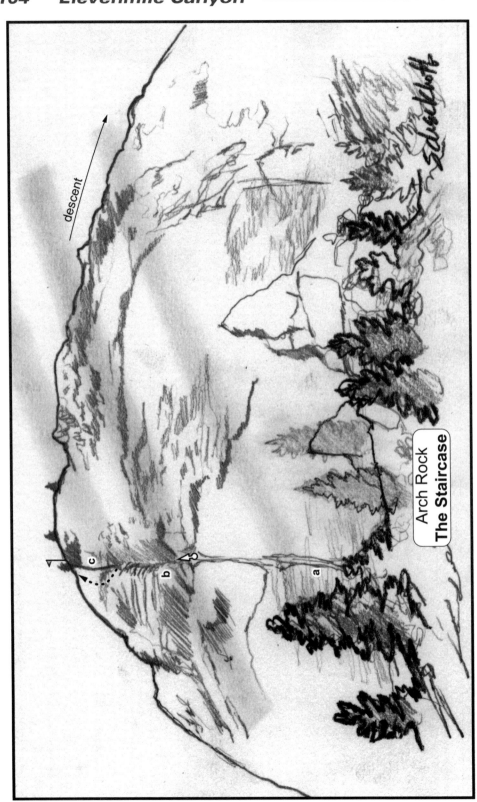

Arch Rock
The Staircase

Arch Rock

This beautiful crag faces west, offering morning shade and afternoon sun. The Staircase Route should not be missed! Park off the road at possible pull-offs. Take one of the steep trails to the crag.

THE STAIRCASE 5.5

Pitch 1   5.4

a. Follow cracks in a right-facing corner. You can belay at 50', keeping the pitch short to facilitate communication or because you're a beginning leader and want to ease into things. You can also continue to a belay in the corner where it steepens.

Pitch 2   5.5

b. Climb the steeper corner. Stemming is a relaxing and graceful way to climb, if you hadn't already noticed . . .

c. Near the top you'll confront a crack that is too large to "fist jam" and too small to "chimney." Cracks of this size are called "offwidths." Though seemingly innocuous, offwidths often embroil the climber in a prolonged, masochistic and noisy struggle (See Huston Crack, page 45). This particular specimen goes at 5.8, though to the modern climber, offwidth ratings may seem a little skewed. Some climbers will go to great lengths to avoid offwidths. With the advent and availability of modern offwidth gear, however, these cracks have become less feared. If aren't well equipped or for any reason, you can avoid this one by climbing around to the left (and perhaps return to lead this "OW" later). Better yet, toprope it, arming yourself with the skills you'll need for future offwidth encounters. Whether you like it or not, offwidths are a cherished part of many great climbs.

Descent: Walk off to the south.

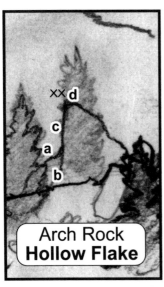

Arch Rock
Hollow Flake

Hollow Flake 5.6 ❖

This one-pitch gem might have been named after the classic pitch on El Capitan's Salathe Wall—but probably wasn't.

a. Angle in from the far left to join the main left-facing corner, or try one of the following variations listed under "b".

b. There are two "direct start" variations, one up the overhanging flake and the other in the corner directly beneath the main corner. Though both go at about 5.7, they are problematic to protect.

c. Glide up the corner. The crux comes when the finger locks get thinner for a move.

d. Belay at a two-bolt anchor.

Descent: Rappel from the two-bolt anchor, about 60' to the ground.

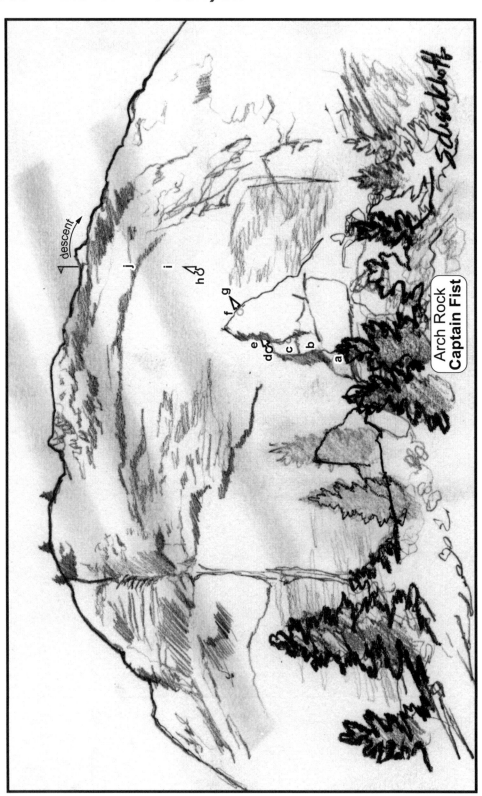

Schießhütte

Arch Rock
Captain Fist

descent

CAPTAIN FIST 5.8

This steep and splendid crack can be done alone as a one-pitch climb or linked with other climbs to reach the summit of Arch Rock.

Pitch 1   5.8

a. Start in an alcove at the bottom of the prominent left-facing corner. The opening sequence involves some unprotected 5.6 moves into the bottom of the corner in order to place a large cam. The moves gaining the cam placement will probably differ from the actual moves you'll make to gain the corner itself.

b. Continue up the corner and onto the shelf on the right wall.

c. Layback and jam up the steep, aesthetic crack.

d. A belay here should prevent the second from swinging into the corner. A fixed rappel anchor lets you return to the ground easily by a single-rope rappel

Pitch 2   5.6

e. Climb the short flared corner above. If you're planning on continuing to the top of Arch Rock, belay a little ways down the right side of the Tilted Tower. Communication between climbers on opposite sides of the Tilted Tower is difficult—try yelling through the crack behind the tower!

Pitch 3   5.7

f. I recommend saving the Arch Rock Direct (5.7 R), which ascends directly above the Tilted Tower, for another day. Instead, traverse right (5.5 R) to a thin crack that takes small nuts.

g. Step right to a knobby quartz dike and climb up to a 3/8" bolt. This is the upper part of a route called Zendance.

h. Angle up and right to a 2-bolt anchor. You can either rappel 100' from here or continue to the top. If you're using a single 60-meter rope for the rappel, equalize the two halves carefully and remember to tie "stopper knots" in the ends.

Pitch 4   5.7 R

i. Climb up enjoyable but unprotected 5.3 to reach the barrier roof and find the small crack that, together with the large crack beneath the roof, offers pro for the moves into the scoop.

j. Though "bouldery," the moves into the scoop go at roughly 5.7. An easier sequence up and slightly left goes at 5.6, a fall from which would slap you down onto the slab beneath the roof. As such, I've added the "R" to the rating. You can stand comfortably and study this sequence until you feel confident. If said confidence fails to arrive, you could reverse the "barrier roof" moves, albeit gracelessly.

Descent: Walk off to the south.

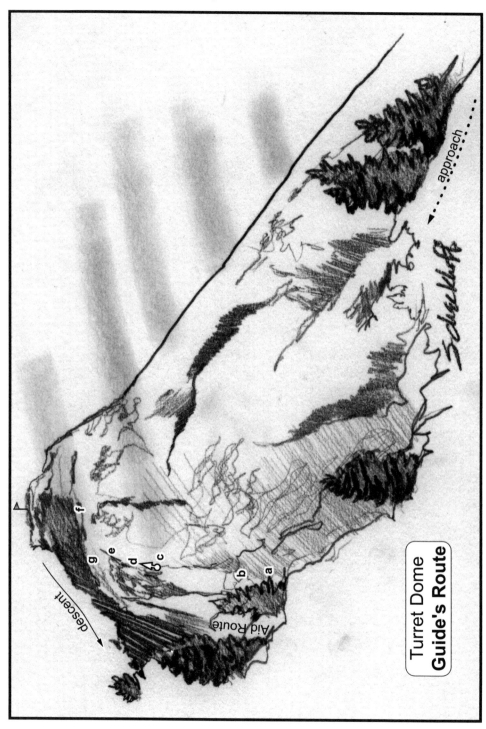

approach

Schwerkraft

descent

Aid Route

f

g   e
     d   c

b   a

Turret Dome
Guide's Route

Turret Dome

The routes on this crag generally face south and west and range from long slab climbs to a few steeper cracks and faces. Park at the Elevenmile Picnic Area, cross the bridge, and follow a climbers' trail to the base.

GUIDE'S ROUTE 5.6

Pitch 1   5.6

a. Find a right-facing corner system with parallel cracks. Climb the left crack as it gently steepens to the crux at 40', just below an old, fixed ring-piton.

b. At the piton step right into the now-singular crack. Follow it until the angle eases and you reach a belay stance where this crack ends and another begins. You can also belay right above the ring-piton if you want to stay in close contact with your partner.

c. If need be, you can retreat from here by leaving some gear and rappelling down and over to another anchor on the "ridge" to the northwest.

Pitch 2   5.4

d. Ascend the small left-facing corner above by face climbing next to it.

e. Once at another, steeper right-facing corner follow either the crack (where you'll find protection) or run it out on easier "tub-climbing" to the right. Aim for a crack up and right, where you can set a good belay anchor.

Pitch 3   5.6/5.7

f. If you want to press on to the summit then cast off on one of the many variations that breach the rooflet above. Weave from ledge to ledge, stringing together little bouldering moves as you go. Though tedious, this process will earn you a fine summit—always a good reward.

g. If the prospects above do not appeal or the weather turns bad, your easiest escape is to traverse left on the low-angle slabs.

Descent: Scramble down to the north.

Within walking distance of the Spillway Campground is a plethora of excellent rock for bouldering and fifth-class climbing. You could happily spend a couple of days here without once setting foot in your car! Potential for hundreds of possible climbs, none listed in any guidebook, can be found in this zone. These routes can be adventurous but not excessively serious provided they offer good anchors. Scrambling around to the top of a 100' formation and dropping a rope on a mystery climb can be a lot of fun!

Although I have not climbed it, the "Aid Route" (5.10a) around to the left of the Guide's Route sounds like a good chance to practice aid climbing, a topic touched on earlier in this book. Consider leading this awkward pitch on aid then lowering down and cleaning it. Finish off by toproping it as a free-climb!

Sport Climbing

Sport climbing evolved out of traditional climbing for three reasons.

One was safety. Relying on clean gear only, certain routes would be horrifically run-out (and many still are). Sometimes these runout sections have technical cruxes in them. One example is The Bulge in Eldorado, where the bolt protecting the crux 5.7 traverse was actually placed on rappel by Layton Kor in 1957 after he had already led the route.

The second reason was that sport climbing opened up chossy or otherwise unprotectable sections of rock on cliffs neglected by trad climbers. In the Front Range, certain cliffs in Boulder and Clear Creek Canyons fall into this category. In Europe, countless acres of crack-free limestone have been systematically bolted over the last 20 years, producing destination climbing areas.

The third reason was convenience. With sport climbing you can lead pitch after pitch without spending time and effort fiddling in RPs, nuts and cams, or messing around with route-finding. The climbing experience is thus simplified, permitting you to concentrate on just "doing the moves."

Sport climbing is not the subject of this book.

Index

Y